CAST IRON SKILLET
BIG FLAVORS

90 Recipes for the Best Pan in Your Kitchen

Sharon Kramis & Julie Kramis Hearne

SASQUATCH BOOKS
SEATTLE

Printed in Canada
Published by Sasquatch Books
17 16 15 14 13 12 11   9 8 7 6 5 4 3 2 1

Cover and interior photographs: Alex Hayden
Cover recipe: Lemon Chicken Sofrito, page 79
Cover and interior design and composition: Kate Basart/Union Pageworks

Library of Congress Cataloging-in-Publication Data is available.

ISBN-13: 978-1-57061-740-9
ISBN-10: 1-57061-740-6

SASQUATCH BOOKS
119 South Main Street, Suite 400 | Seattle, WA 98104 | 206.467.4300
www.sasquatchbooks.com | custserv@sasquatchbooks.com

CAST IRON SKILLET
BIG FLAVORS

For everyone who shares our passion for cast iron, we hope this book will continue to inspire you to explore more great recipes and big flavors in the cast iron skillet.
—S. K. and J. K. H.

contents

acknowledgments

Thank you to my wonderful daughter, Julie, who let me join her on the culinary journey along the spice trail. A special thanks to my husband, Larry, for accepting without ever knowing what was going to be for dinner. To Barbara Hinck, taster, friend, and computer wizard. To Anthony's Homeport Restaurants for their continued commitment to the best of the Northwest. To our sons Joe and Tom, who still love to drop in for a family dinner.   —S. K.

To my coauthor, mom, and friend! You have taught me not only how to cook, but how things should taste. To my husband, Harker, and my three boys, Reilly, Konrad, and Andrew, who never know what's for dinner but through this book have gained a more adventurous palate. Thanks, boys, for your patience and open minds.   —J. K. H.

We would like to thank our editors—Gary Luke, Rachelle Longé, and Kristi Hein—and everyone at Sasquatch Books for continuing on the cast iron skillet journey with us.

We would also like to thank Alex Hayden, our food photographer, who works magic with the camera, and Christy Nordstrom, our food stylist, who knows how to make food look delicious and natural with her finishing touches.   —S. K. and J. K. H.

A NOTE TO OUR READERS

We wanted to write *Cast Iron Skillet Big Flavors* because, thanks to the culinary influences we describe in this book, we've been spicing up our recipes. What we cooked five years ago, we may choose to spice up today. The availability of world spices, condiments, and sauces has made it easier to cook outside our comfort zone. We have traveled to new countries and returned home to re-create these flavors in our own kitchens.

Our skillets still remain our favorite pans in the kitchen. They can take the place of a tava (or tawa) or a wok. We find that not only do we use one skillet, but sometimes we use two or three at a time. We can cook our main dish in one and a side dish in another. As we began our journey of exploring big flavors, we soon realized the depth of knowledge that is available from cookbook authors who have lived and explored these cuisines deeply and translated them. We are just beginning our exploration, and we'd like you to share our journey in exploring new flavors and new dishes.

Today's cooks lead very busy lives, and we need recipes that are not too time-consuming, with lots of good flavors. To that end, we offer recipes that are both simplified and flexible, using spice blends and sauces that you can either create from scratch when time allows, or buy when time is short.

We hope you will enjoy this book as much as you did the first.

introduction

WE STILL BELIEVE THE CAST IRON SKILLET IS THE BEST PAN IN YOUR KITCHEN. IN our home it currently lives on top of the stove or in the oven. Yes, it is heavy and a little hard to clean at times, but worth the trouble. There are many things that you can cook and bake in the skillet that you can't do in any other pan. The cast iron skillet is unique for its ability to provide dry, even heat. Its porous surface prevents excess moisture in the pan. The benefit is that you get even browning and beautiful crusting. We like that you can go from searing on the stove top to finishing in the oven in the same pan. Since our last book, we have found that we are adding much more spice to our cooking. Our kitchen is a melting pot of different flavors. Our pantries are filled with condiments from around the world. Today sriracha sauce (Thai hot sauce) is becoming as popular as ketchup in many homes. The influence of new world cuisines in our grocery stores and restaurants has made a huge impact on the way we are cooking today. We may crave pho instead of chicken noodle soup or an Indian curry instead of a beef stew. In the 1960s, French cooking was very influential, using lots of butter and cream. Julia Child started our passion for cooking. In the 1980s, Asian influences inspired us through travel and eating out. Today the Food Network brings us a new cuisine every half hour. Now these influences are inspiring us to lean more toward cooking with chilies, spice blends, and Asian sauces and condiments. We are no longer afraid of world flavors. We are inspired to explore new recipes. We can use our skillet for stir-frying and baking. We want to use these flavors in our own kitchens and cook new recipes with big flavors for our family and friends. We hope you will find this the beginning of your spice trail and fill your pantry with new flavors.

your cast iron pan

CAST IRON COOKWARE HAS BEEN AROUND FOR HUNDREDS OF years. Centuries ago, cast iron kettles and skillets were used over open fires in Europe. They were some of the very few treasured items that settlers brought with them to the New World. ⫯ Cast iron pans are formed through the process of sand-casting. Molten iron is poured into a sand-clay mold of the desired shape. After it cools, the mold is removed and the pan's surface is smoothed by a stone-washing process. Although pioneer cast iron companies Griswold Manufacturing and Wagner Manufacturing are no longer in business, you can occasionally discover their pans at second-hand stores. They are a great find. Well-seasoned and well-used, they are our favorites. ⫯ Today's cast iron pans come in a wide variety of shapes and sizes to suit almost any culinary need. We recommend pans from Lodge Manufacturing that are made in the United States. Founded in 1896, Lodge is the largest domestic producer of high-quality iron cookware. Their pieces range from skillets, Dutch ovens, grill pans, and griddles to specialty pans for breads, casseroles, and muffins. Lodge products are readily available in cookware shops and hardware stores throughout the country. French-made Le Creuset's enamel-coated cast iron cookware, which is more expensive than traditional cast iron, is our favorite for soups and casseroles. Staub cast iron, also made in France, includes unique pieces sold in many different shapes and sizes. Both Le Creuset and Staub are available at specialty cookware stores such as Sur La Table (see Resources, page 143). ⫯ Often, cooks who are unfamiliar with cast iron are pleasantly surprised to find that well-seasoned cast iron has a perfect nonstick surface. Teflon-coated and stainless steel pans tend to cause food to "sweat," which stews and toughens meat instead of browning it, and prevents a crisp crust from forming. Food cooked in cast iron doesn't sweat due to the pan's porous surface. Cast iron pans heat quickly and evenly and maintain their heat. They provide an even exchange of heat with the food, thus allowing meats to brown and caramelize, staying tender. The high heat of the pan forms golden crusts on baked goods and acts just like a wood-fired oven for pizzas and breads. ⫯ Cast iron's versatility is what appeals to us the most. We use our cast iron skillets for pan-searing, pan-roasting, stir-frying, and baking. We find that an iron skillet is an excellent alternative to a wok—especially for those who cook on an electric stove. For camping, cast iron pans are indispensable. A Dutch oven is perfect for cooking over an outdoor fire, and it can be used as either an oven or a slow cooker.

PURCHASING CAST IRON COOKWARE

Today most new pans come preseasoned, which means you can use them right out of the box. Even a preseasoned pan, however, will need to be reseasoned now and then to maintain its nonstick surface. Unseasoned new pans are gunmetal gray in color, but with proper care and much use they will develop the familiar black patina that is the hallmark of a well-seasoned skillet.

You have a lot of choices when shopping for a new cast iron pan. Keep in mind that you don't need every shape and size. We own 8-, 10-, and 12-inch skillets—two with straight 2-inch sides for searing and roasting, and one with 4-inch sides for stewing and braising. We love our griddle pan for pancakes, bacon, and eggs cooked side by side. A grill pan is our indoor barbecue, perfect for grilling meats of all kinds.

Here are descriptions of our favorite skillets and pans. Note that most cast iron skillets do not come with lids. When we are in need of a lid, we use one from our cupboards that is the same size as the pan.

Skillets are generally straight sided and long handled, and range in size from 6½ inches in diameter and 1¼ inches deep to 15¼ inches in diameter and 2¼ inches deep. (Sizes are indicated on the bottom of the skillet.) Large skillets have loop handles on either side, which make them easier to manage.

Lodge also has a stir-fry skillet, which resembles a wok and is 12¾ inches in diameter and 3¼ inches deep. If you like wok cookery, you'll find that this cast iron version works well on both electric and gas ranges.

Grill pans, both round and square, have raised ridges in the bottom of the pan, which make them ideal for cooking boneless, skinless chicken breasts, fish fillets, and steaks indoors. These pans are a wonderful alternative to an outdoor grill. Sizes range from 9 inches in diameter to about 11 inches in diameter; they are approximately 2 inches deep.

Dutch ovens have loop handles and always come with lids. They are approximately 4 to 5 inches deep and range in capacity from 5 quarts to 9 quarts. Note that Dutch ovens differ from "camp ovens" or "spiders." Camp ovens are deep like Dutch ovens but have three legs for setting on an open fire. (Dutch ovens have flat bottoms.) We have become reacquainted with our Dutch oven, and we use it indoors as well as outdoors. Lodge makes a great preseasoned, 6-quart Dutch oven perfect for stews and soups.

Griddles are flat with smooth surfaces. Some have grill ridges on one side. Our favorite is rectangular and fits over two burners.

You will also find specialty cast iron pans used for specific recipes. The specialty pans we own are a popover pan, an ebelskiver pan, and a Swedish pancake pan. Season specialty cookware as you would any other cast iron pan, and always use a little butter or vegetable oil before adding batter.

SEASONING NEW CAST IRON AND RESEASONING OLD

The secret to successful cooking in cast iron is properly seasoning and caring for your pans. The point of seasoning is to bake the oil into the pan's porous surface to create a smooth nonstick coating and to prevent rust. Most new cast iron pans come preseasoned and can be used right out of the box; those gunmetal gray pans with sticky residue are nearly obsolete. The instructions below will help you season and maintain any cast iron pan.

To reseason old or never-seasoned cast iron, follow these steps:

1. Preheat the oven to 375°F.

2. Wash your pan with warm soapy water (only use soap when reseasoning) and scrub with a stiff brush or steel wool. Rinse with warm water, removing any sticky coating. Dry completely with a kitchen towel.

3. Rub the pan inside and out with a thin coat of vegetable shortening; this will melt into the pan's porous surface when heated.

4. Place the pan upside down on a baking sheet lined with foil, and bake for 1 hour. Let it cool completely, then store with a paper towel inside.

If your seasoned pan starts to stick, follow these steps for maintaining your cast iron:

1. Heat your pan on the stove top over medium heat. Rub the entire inside of the pan with olive or vegetable oil, using a wad of paper towels to distribute the oil evenly. Wipe out any excess oil and repeat three or four more times. This heating process expands the iron's porous surface and allows the oil to soak in.

2. Turn off the heat and let the pan cool completely.

THE DO'S AND DON'TS FOR CLEANING AND CARING FOR CAST IRON

Don't ever wash a skillet in a dishwasher! Sometimes, especially after cooking egg dishes, you will have to briefly soak the skillet before scrubbing.

Don't use metal utensils to scrape the pan.

To clean and care for a skillet after each use, do the following:

1. Hold the pan under hot water and scrub it clean with a nylon scrub pad. You may need to eliminate strong flavors that have permeated the pan's porous surface (for example, after sautéing onions for a long time); in this case, scrub the pan with 1 tablespoon each coarse salt and olive oil, then wipe clean.

2. After rinsing, dry the skillet on the stove top over medium heat. Turn off the heat after it has warmed through, and add 2 tablespoons olive or vegetable oil, wiping the oil over the entire inside of the pan with a wad of paper towels.

3. Cool, then line the pan with a paper towel and store in a warm, dry place. Store lids separately.

Note: If you find a rusted cast iron pan at an antique shop or garage sale, you *can* rescue it. Simply wash it in hot water with a few drops of dishwashing soap (it is okay to use a little soap if you are reseasoning) or a mild abrasive such as coarse salt and olive oil, then scour the pan with a stiff brush or steel wool. Follow the seasoning directions on the previous page before using.

COOKING WITH CAST IRON

Cast iron heats very evenly, so you don't need to cook at high temperatures. Most of the time we use medium heat.

Remember that the handles of cast iron pans get hot, so keep oven mitts close by when using a skillet. Because the pans are heavy, always use two hands (and two oven mitts!) when lifting a hot skillet. Cast iron stays hot long after it has been removed from the heat, so remember to use a trivet when placing your pan on a table or countertop.

When you are ready to cook, heat your skillet over medium heat before adding food to the pan. To test the heat, sprinkle in a few drops of water; when the pan is ready for cooking, the droplets will dance across the pan. Foods are less likely to stick if your pan is very hot.

Don't store food in a cast iron skillet, because the pan may impart a metallic taste.

Cast iron pans do demand a bit of care, but once you've cooked in one, we're certain you will agree that they are well worth the effort.

pantry staples
our favorite things

In addition to the usual suspects, these are our must-haves in the kitchen:

NON-PERISHABLES

Anchovies or anchovy paste
Arborio rice
Balsamic vinegar
Black bean paste
Black rice wine vinegar
Canned albacore tuna
Chili garlic paste
Chipotle chilies in adobo sauce
Cider vinegar
Coconut milk
Dried fruit: cherries, dates, prunes
Dried mushrooms
Dried or canned beans:
    black, cannellini, garbanzo,
    pinto, refried
Dried pasilla peppers
Dried pasta
Dry sherry
Hatch green chiles
Hazelnut oil
Herdez Salsa Verde
Hoisin sauce
Honey
Hot sauce, preferably Crystal brand
Marsala
More Than Gourmet veal demi-glace
Muir Glen fire-roasted tomatoes
Nuts
Olive oil
Oyster sauce
Panko bread crumbs
Pernod

Red wine vinegar
Rice: brown, white
Rice wine vinegar
Sesame oil
Sherry vinegar
Stocks or bouillon cubes:
    beef, chicken, vegetable
Sweet chili sauce
Truffle oil
Walnut oil
Worcestershire sauce

PERISHABLES

Capers
Chutney
Fish sauce
Gourmet Garden fresh ginger paste,
    lemongrass paste, and dill herb
    blend
Miso paste
Mrs. Renfro's Pickled Jalapeño
    Peppers
Olives: green and picholine or
    kalamata
Ponzu sauce (regular or citrus)
Soy sauce
Sriracha sauce
Tamarind paste
Tiger sauce
Wasabi paste
XO sauce

SPICES AND BLENDS

Aleppo pepper
Arabic baharat
Besar
Cardamom
Chinese five-spice blend
Dukkah
Fennel seeds
Furikake
Garam masala (see page 56)
Harissa
Poudre de Colombo
Ras el hanout
Saffron
Shichimi togarashi
    ("Seven Flavor Chili Pepper")
Star anise
Syrian zahtar
Urfa biber
Vanilla beans

breakfast
anytime

Smoked Salmon Hash with Tricolored Potatoes
Chilaquiles
Skillet Quiche with Broccoli, Mushrooms, and Green Onions
Croque Monsieur Meets Croque Madame
Apple French Toast Bread Pudding
Papas con Chorizo
Crumpets
Green Chili Soufflé with Dungeness Crab
Blueberry Sour Cream Coffee Cake
Cornmeal Skillet Cakes
South African Bobotie
Skillet-Roasted Granola with Candied Pecans, Craisins, and Coconut
Brioche French Toast
Chanterelle and Gruyère Strata with Fresh Thyme
German Apple Pancake

WEDNESDAY NIGHT IS OUR NIGHT TO FIX AN EASY BREAKFAST FOR DINNER. THE German Apple Pancake served with sausages, or Croque Monsieur Meets Croque Madame, made on crispy sourdough bread, are a nice change from a traditional dinner. Simple, satisfying, and delicious.  Sunday morning family breakfast is a good time to sit down together and recap the week and what's coming up. Stay in your pajamas and have a second cup of coffee and a glass of freshly squeezed orange juice while you anticipate Blueberry Sour Cream Coffee Cake baking in the skillet. Crisp bacon sizzles on top of the stove while a bowl of fresh berries sits on the table. You can spice up breakfast with Papas con Chorizo and Chilaquiles, which are a nice change from bacon and eggs. Eggs of any kind taste better with a dash of your favorite hot sauce. Our family also loves to make the Skillet-Roasted Granola with Candied Pecans, Craisins, and Coconut. It makes a perfect snack, or serve it with a bowl of fresh fruit. On a Saturday or Sunday afternoon, invite a friend over to enjoy a cup of tea and Crumpets. A cast iron skillet and breakfast go hand in hand. Whether it's pancakes, bacon, sausage, French toast, or hash browns, breakfast from a skillet tastes wonderful and looks so inviting.

smoked salmon hash with tricolored potatoes

Tricolored potatoes—a mixture of red, blue or purple, and yellow varieties—make for a colorful Sunday breakfast dish that goes well with oven-baked crisp bacon and coffee cake. This versatile recipe is open to variations; you can substitute leftover pot roast, corned beef, or chicken for the smoked salmon. If you choose to substitute another meat, chop it into small pieces and add to the skillet with the potatoes.

. . . .

MAKES 6 SERVINGS

- In a medium saucepan, cover the potatoes with cold water. Bring to a boil, then turn down heat and cook until potatoes are fork tender, about 10 minutes. Drain and cool slightly, then coarsely chop.

- In a 10- or 12-inch skillet, melt the butter, add the onions, and cook for 3 to 5 minutes. Add the olive oil and the chopped potatoes and cook over medium heat until the potatoes are lightly browned, about 8 minutes. Add the apple, chilies, and cream. Continue to cook for 5 minutes and remove from heat. Break the salmon into 2-inch pieces and place on top of the potatoes. Sprinkle with parsley, salt, and pepper; top with sour cream and green onions; and serve.

2 pounds small tricolored potatoes or small Red Bliss potatoes

3 tablespoons unsalted butter

1 cup chopped yellow onion

3 tablespoons olive oil

½ cup chopped apple, skin on

¼ cup chopped roasted poblano chili or canned green Hatch chilies

¼ cup heavy cream

8 ounces smoked salmon

¼ cup chopped parsley

Salt and freshly ground black pepper

Sour cream, for topping (optional)

Chopped green onions, for topping (optional)

chilaquiles

This is our easy version of chilaquiles, a very popular Mexican breakfast or brunch dish. In this recipe, we use Italian sausage instead of chorizo. If using chorizo, be sure to remove from casing and cook until all the fat is released and the meat begins to brown and crisp. Drain well on paper towels. The tortilla strips sold in grocery stores work perfectly for this recipe. You can find green salsa and taco sauce in the Mexican or ethnic food aisle of most supermarkets, and Cotija cheese and Mexican crema in the dairy section. You can also serve this with shredded chicken on top.

. . . .

MAKES 4 SERVINGS

- Preheat the broiler to high.

- In a small saucepan, heat the beans over low heat, stirring, until hot. Set aside.

- Heat a 10- to 12-inch skillet over medium heat, then add the sausage and cook, breaking it up with a wooden spoon, until golden brown, about 10 minutes. Transfer to a plate. In the same skillet, distribute the tortilla strips. Sprinkle the cooked sausage over the top. Add the salsa verde, then drizzle with the red taco sauce. Sprinkle with the cheese blend, then sprinkle over ¼ cup of the Cotija cheese. Place under the broiler to melt the cheese and heat the sauce, 3 to 5 minutes. Remove as soon as cheese has melted.

- Meanwhile, in a medium bowl, whisk the eggs with the milk until combined. Stir in the salt and pepper.

8 ounces (½ can) refried or black beans

½ pound spicy or mild Italian sausage

1 (3.5-ounce) bag tortilla strips

1 (7-ounce) can Herdez Salsa Verde or green enchilada sauce

¼ cup Herdez Salsa Taquera or other taco sauce

¾ cup grated Mexican cheese blend (Monterey Jack and mild cheddar cheese)

½ cup grated Cotija cheese, queso fresco, or feta, divided

4 large eggs, beaten

2 tablespoons milk

¼ teaspoon salt

⅛ teaspoon freshly ground black pepper

2 teaspoons unsalted butter

1 tablespoon chopped fresh cilantro

½ cup diced avocado

½ cup diced white onion

¼ cup sour cream or Mexican crema

3 tablespoons fresh cilantro leaves, for garnish (optional)

- Melt the butter in a nonstick pan over medium-low heat. Add the egg mixture and let set for 20 seconds. With a wooden spoon or silicone spatula, stir the eggs and cook for 3 minutes or until no longer runny.

- Divide the chilaquiles among 4 plates and sprinkle each serving with the remaining Cotija cheese, cilantro, avocado, and onion. Serve with a quarter of the scrambled eggs, refried beans, and a dollop of sour cream, then sprinkle with cilantro leaves.

skillet quiche with broccoli, mushrooms, and green onions

This is a great way to get children to eat their vegetables. Vegetables that are cooked with eggs and cheese–who wouldn't love it? The skillet provides dry, even heat, so the crust becomes golden and the filling is light and creamy. Serve anytime of the day–with fresh fruit for breakfast or a salad for lunch.

Note: This piecrust recipe would typically yield two crusts, but you will need the extra dough for the deeper skillet.

. . . .

MAKES 6 TO 8 SERVINGS

- To prepare the piecrust, in a large bowl, combine the flour, salt, and sugar. Add the butter and, working quickly, using your fingers or a pastry knife, mix until it resembles coarse crumbs. Add the ice water 1 to 2 tablespoons at a time to the flour, mixing gently with your hands after each addition, until the dough just comes together. Do not overmix. Once all the liquid is incorporated, form into a flattened disk and wrap with plastic wrap. Chill for at least 30 minutes and up to 1 day.

- Preheat the oven to 375°F. Remove the dough from the refrigerator and let it warm up slightly. On a lightly floured surface, roll out the dough large enough (at least 14 inches across) to fit in the skillet and halfway up the sides. Fold the crust over the rolling pin and carefully transfer to the skillet. Gently press the crust into the skillet to fit evenly. Line the crust with foil, add about 4 cups dried beans, and bake for 15 minutes. Remove from the oven; keep the oven on if you will be proceeding immediately with the

PIECRUSTS

2½ cups all-purpose flour

1 teaspoon salt

2 teaspoons sugar

1 cup (2 sticks) cold unsalted butter, cut into pieces

6 to 8 tablespoons ice cold water

QUICHE

½ pound Italian sausage, casing removed

1 tablespoon unsalted butter

1 cup button mushrooms, cleaned, stems removed, and sliced ¼ inch thick (cut in half first if mushrooms are large)

1½ cups bite-size chopped broccoli

6 large eggs

1½ cups half-and-half

1 teaspoon kosher salt or sea salt, divided

⅛ teaspoon freshly ground black pepper

⅛ teaspoon nutmeg

¼ cup finely chopped green onion, green part only

⅔ cup shredded cheddar cheese

⅔ cup shredded Monterey Jack cheese

rest of the recipe. With a medium bowl close by, carefully lift out the foil with hot beans and transfer to the bowl. Pick out any beans left in the crust and set the crust aside.

- If the oven is not already on, preheat to 375°F. To prepare the filling, in a 10- to 12-inch cast iron skillet, cook the sausage, breaking it up into small pieces, until nicely browned. Transfer to a bowl, leaving some of the drippings in the pan, and set aside. Add to the pan the butter and mushrooms. Cook over medium heat for 5 minutes, stirring occasionally. Add the broccoli and cook for 7 minutes more. Return the sausage to the pan and stir.

- In a medium bowl, whisk together the eggs, half-and-half, ½ teaspoon salt, pepper, and nutmeg. Spread the sausage mixture and the green onion evenly over the bottom of the piecrust. Sprinkle with half of the cheeses, pour the egg mixture over the cheese, then top with the rest of the cheese. Bake until the top is golden and the center is firm, 35 to 45 minutes.

- Sprinkle with the remaining ½ teaspoon salt and allow to cool slightly before cutting into wedges.

croque monsieur meets croque madame

Croque means "to crunch" and monsieur means "mister." We love this "crunchy mister" for its wonderful Mornay sauce. The Croque Madame adds a fried egg, and we've found that the combination is a big hit with both kids and adults. In our version we've placed the sauce inside the sandwich, which makes it easier to eat.

· · · · · · · · · · · · · · · · · ·

MAKES 4 SERVINGS

- Place the Gruyère and Parmesan in a medium bowl and sprinkle with the flour. Toss to coat the cheeses with the flour and set aside.

- In a medium saucepan, melt the 3 tablespoons butter over medium-low heat.

- Add the cheese-flour mixture to the butter and stir. Add the milk and stir until the sauce comes together and starts to thicken, about 5 minutes. Turn the heat down to low. Add the nutmeg, ground mustard, paprika, salt, and pepper and stir. Remove from the heat and set aside.

- Lightly toast the bread in a toaster or on a baking sheet under the broiler. For each sandwich, spread 1 tablespoon mayonnaise and ½ teaspoon mustard on one slice of toast; leave the other dry.

- Preheat the broiler. Heat a 10- or 12-inch cast iron skillet over medium heat. Add the ham slices and cook for 10 seconds on each side. Transfer to a plate. Place the ham on top of the mayonnaise-and-mustard-covered toasts. Spread 3 tablespoons of the Mornay sauce evenly

EASY MORNAY SAUCE

1 cup grated Gruyère

¼ cup freshly grated Parmesan cheese

2 tablespoons all-purpose flour

3 tablespoons unsalted butter

¾ cup milk

⅛ teaspoon freshly ground nutmeg

¼ teaspoon ground mustard

¼ teaspoon paprika

¼ teaspoon salt

⅛ teaspoon freshly ground white pepper

SANDWICH

8 slices French or sourdough bread

8 tablespoons mayonnaise

1 tablespoon plus 1 teaspoon Dijon mustard

4 slices smoked ham

½ cup grated Gruyère or cheddar cheese

5 tablespoons unsalted butter, at room temperature, divided

4 extra-large eggs

3 tablespoons water

Salt and freshly ground black pepper

Fresh fruit, for garnish

Fresh mint leaves, for garnish

Honey, for drizzling

over the dry piece of toast and sprinkle with 2 tablespoons grated cheese. Repeat with the remaining 3 pieces of dry toast. Place these sauce side down on a baking sheet and place under the broiler until light golden brown, 3 to 4 minutes. Set aside.

- In a nonstick pan, melt 1 tablespoon butter over medium-low heat. Add the water to the pan. Once hot, break in the eggs, one at a time; cover and cook until yolks are set and whites are completely cooked, 3 to 5 minutes. With a spatula, gently flip the eggs one at a time and cook for another 10 seconds. Place the eggs on top of the ham and season with salt and pepper. Top each egg with the Mornay toast.

- Melt 1 tablespoon butter in a 10- or 12-inch cast iron skillet over medium heat. Add 2 or 3 sandwiches at a time, gently pressing down with a spatula, and cook for 3 minutes. While they cook, lightly butter the top of each sandwich with about 1 teaspoon of the softened butter. Flip the sandwiches over and cook for 3 minutes more, pressing down gently with the back of the spatula. Remove to a cutting board. Cook the other sandwiches the same way, cut all the sandwiches in half, and serve with fresh fruit, fresh mint, and a drizzle of honey.

apple french toast bread pudding

This makes a delicious breakfast, served with crispy bacon or sausage and fresh orange juice. Sometimes we just crumble the bacon right on top!

. . . .

MAKES 8 SERVINGS

- To prepare the apples, melt the butter in a 10- or 12-inch cast iron skillet over medium heat. Add the apples, ¼ teaspoon of the cinnamon, and ½ cup of the sugar and sauté for 5 minutes. Add the water and cook until caramelized, about 5 more minutes. Transfer from the skillet to a bowl and set aside.

- To prepare the bread pudding, in a large bowl, beat the eggs, half-and-half, remaining granulated sugar, brown sugar, nutmeg, remaining cinnamon, cardamom, orange zest, and vanilla together until blended and the eggs are well combined. Rub the clean skillet all over with the softened butter. Lay half of the bread strips flat in the skillet, sprinkle with half of the apple mixture, then top with the remaining bread slices. Cover the other half of the apple mixture and refrigerate. Pour the egg mixture over the bread and press down with the back of a spatula to make sure the bread soaks up the egg mixture. Cover with foil and refrigerate for 1 to 2 hours.

2 tablespoons unsalted butter

4 apples, peeled, cored, and diced into ½-inch pieces

¾ teaspoon ground cinnamon, divided

¾ cup granulated sugar, divided

¼ cup water

6 large eggs

1½ cups half-and-half

¼ cup brown sugar

¼ teaspoon freshly ground nutmeg

¼ teaspoon ground cardamom (optional)

2 teaspoons orange zest

1 teaspoon vanilla extract

2 tablespoons unsalted butter, at room temperature

10 to 12 slices French bread, thick sliced, crust removed, cut into 4-inch strips

Warm maple syrup, for serving

¼ cup heavy cream, for serving

- Preheat the oven to 375°F.

- Remove the pan and the reserved apple mixture from the refrigerator and let sit at room temperature for 15 minutes before baking. Leaving the foil on, bake the bread pudding for 30 minutes. Remove the foil and bake until golden on top and somewhat firm in the center, about 25 minutes more.

- Ten minutes before the bread pudding is finished, add the reserved apple mixture to a small saucepan and cook over medium heat until hot.

- Cut the bread pudding into wedges, and top with the warm apple mixture, warm maple syrup, and a light drizzle of cream.

papas con chorizo

These quite spicy potatoes are the centerpiece of a weekend brunch. We like to serve them with scrambled eggs and coffee cake. It's important to use Mexican chorizo, not Spanish, as the two are quite different: Mexican chorizo is spicier and needs to be cooked before eating.

. . . .

MAKES 4 TO 6 SERVINGS

- Cook the potatoes in boiling salted water just until tender, 10 to 12 minutes. Drain.

- In a 12-inch cast iron skillet, cook the chorizo over medium-low heat for 5 to 8 minutes. To soak up the extra oil from the sausage, simply blot lightly with paper towels. Add the butter and white onion to the pan and cook for 5 minutes. Add the potatoes and cook, stirring, until the potatoes are well blended with the sausage, 6 to 8 minutes. Top with a dollop of sour cream, sprinkle with the green onions, and serve.

1½ pounds small red potatoes, cut in quarters

6 ounces uncooked Mexican chorizo, removed from casing

2 tablespoons unsalted butter

½ cup diced white onion

½ cup sour cream, for topping

½ cup chopped green onions, for topping

crumpets

Many crumpet recipes call for yeast, but in this one the cream of tartar, baking soda, and buttermilk create an active, bubbly batter. Some recipes use molds to form a perfect circle, but we like to have different shapes. We can't think of a better match than crumpets and cast iron–except, of course, a cup of your favorite tea. Butter and jam are traditional toppings, but we also like to serve the crumpets sprinkled with cinnamon and sugar.

. . . .

MAKES 12 CRUMPETS

- Sift the flour, sugar, salt, baking soda, and cream of tartar into a medium bowl. Using your fingers, work the cold butter into the flour mixture, until it resembles pea-sized lumps. Make a well in the center of the flour and pour in the eggs and ¼ cup of the buttermilk; whisk well. The flour should gradually come in from the sides and incorporate into the center. Add another ¼ cup of the buttermilk and beat until the dough becomes airy. Add the remaining ½ cup buttermilk and whisk in to blend. Cover and let stand at room temperature for 1 hour.

1¾ cups all-purpose flour
¼ cup sugar
¼ teaspoon salt
½ teaspoon baking soda
1 teaspoon cream of tartar
2 tablespoons cold unsalted butter
2 large eggs, beaten
1 cup buttermilk
2 tablespoons vegetable oil or butter
Butter, jam, or apple butter, for topping

- Lightly oil (using 2 teaspoons oil per batch) a 10- or 12-inch cast iron skillet. Over medium heat, drop spoonfuls of batter, each 2 to 3 tablespoons, into the hot pan and cook until bubbles appear on top. Flip each crumpet over and cook briefly until lightly golden on the bottom. Serve with butter, jam, or apple butter.

green chili soufflé with dungeness crab

This is a nice, light, and creamy brunch dish. When corn is in season, use fresh—there's nothing better! If you can't find Dungeness crab, you can substitute jumbo lump crabmeat.

. . . .

MAKES 6 SERVINGS

- Preheat the oven to 350°F.

- Butter a 10-inch cast iron skillet. Sprinkle half of the cheese evenly in the skillet. Top with chilies, corn, and remaining cheese. Mix the flour and half-and-half until smooth. Mix in the eggs and blend well. Pour the egg mixture over the cheese. Bake until golden brown, about 35 minutes. Place portions on 6 individual plates, top each with 2 tablespoons salsa verde and about 1 ounce crab, and serve immediately.

2 tablespoons unsalted butter

1½ cups grated medium cheddar cheese

1 (4-ounce) can diced green chilies, drained

1 cup canned corn, well drained

2 tablespoons all-purpose flour

1½ cups half-and-half

3 large eggs, lightly beaten

1 (7-ounce) can Embasa salsa verde or other green salsa

½ pound fresh Dungeness crab, for garnish

blueberry sour cream coffee cake

At one of James Beard's cooking classes back in the early 1970s, he had the class prepare a brunch menu. Everyone came back with a menu that included dishes like veal piccata. James took one look at the menu, threw it down, and demanded, "Where are the coffee cakes? Where are the sausages?" Now we always serve coffee cake and sausages for brunch. The cast iron skillet gives this coffee cake a moist interior and a crunchy, golden crust.

MAKES 8 SERVINGS

- Preheat the oven to 325°F and butter a 10-inch cast iron skillet.

- To prepare the topping, combine all the ingredients and mix with your fingers until crumbly.

- Using a mixer, cream together the butter and sugar. Add the eggs, one at a time, and continue beating until light and fluffy.

- In a medium bowl, mix the milk, sour cream, and vanilla together. In another bowl, combine the flour and baking powder. Add the flour mixture alternately with the sour cream-milk mixture to the egg mixture. Fold in the blueberries. Spread the batter in the buttered skillet.

- Sprinkle the topping over the cake and bake for about 45 minutes, or until a wooden skewer inserted in the center comes out clean.

STREUSEL TOPPING
⅔ cup all-purpose flour

½ cup sugar

6 tablespoons unsalted butter

½ teaspoon ground cinnamon

CAKE
½ cup (1 stick) unsalted butter

1 cup sugar

2 extra-large eggs

½ cup milk

1 cup sour cream

1 teaspoon vanilla extract

2 cups all-purpose flour

2 teaspoons baking powder

2 cups fresh blueberries

cornmeal skillet cakes

With the addition of egg whites, these cornmeal cakes are nice and light. You can have them for breakfast with eggs and bacon or make small cakes and serve as an appetizer with pulled pork and mango salsa.

. . . .

MAKES 10 TO 12 CAKES

- In a medium bowl, combine the cornmeal and boiling water. Add the melted butter, sugar, and egg and mix well. In a separate bowl, combine the flour, baking soda, and salt; mix. Add half of the flour mixture and half of the buttermilk to the cornmeal mixture and stir. Add the remaining flour mixture and buttermilk and stir until just incorporated. With a spatula, carefully fold in the egg whites, retaining as much of the volume as possible.

- Heat a 10- or 12-inch cast iron skillet over medium to medium heat. Add the oil and swirl in the pan. Pour in 2 heaping tablespoons batter to form each cake, cooking about 5 at a time. Cook until golden brown, about 3 minutes on each side.

- Serve with warm maple syrup or honey butter.

¾ cup finely ground cornmeal

½ cup boiling water

2 tablespoons unsalted butter, melted

1 tablespoon sugar

1 large egg, beaten

¾ cup all-purpose flour

½ teaspoon baking soda

½ teaspoon kosher salt

½ cup buttermilk or ½ cup milk plus 2 tablespoons sour cream or plain yogurt

2 egg whites, beaten to soft peaks

2 tablespoons vegetable or canola oil

Maple syrup or honey butter, for topping

south african bobotie

This South African dish made with ground beef and egg-bread topping makes for a perfect brunch dish or casual skillet dinner and is unquestionably "comfort food." We suggest serving it with chutney and a fresh fennel, orange, and watercress salad.

. . . .

MAKES 4 SERVINGS

- Preheat the oven to 375°F.

- In a 10-inch cast iron skillet over medium heat, sauté the butter and onions for several minutes. Add the ground beef and cook until the meat is lightly browned. Add the curry powder, water, and dried apricots. Stir in the water-moistened bread crumbs and flatten slightly with a spoon. Beat the egg with the milk and pour evenly over the meat mixture. Dot with the pieces of butter. Transfer to the oven and bake until the top has a light brown crust, about 35 minutes. Serve warm.

2 tablespoons unsalted butter

1½ cups chopped yellow onion

½ pound lean ground beef

1 tablespoon curry powder

¼ cup water

½ cup chopped dried apricots

1 cup fresh bread crumbs, moistened with ½ cup water

2 large eggs

1 cup milk

2 tablespoons unsalted butter, cut into 8 pieces

skillet-roasted granola with candied pecans, craisins, and coconut

Granola sprinkled over Greek yogurt is a welcome breakfast on a busy morning: easy to assemble, easy to eat, and so satisfying. The Craisins and candied pecans in our version take it to a level above ordinary granola—making it an elegant gift for the holidays.

• • • • • • • • • • • • • • • •

MAKES 8 TO 10 SERVINGS

- Preheat the oven to 200°F.

- In a medium bowl, combine the oatmeal, coconut, Craisins, pecans, oil, honey, and cinnamon. Spread evenly in a 12-inch cast iron skillet and roast for 2 hours, stirring every 30 minutes. Sprinkle with the salt. Let cool and dry completely before packaging.

3 cups old-fashioned oatmeal (not instant)

½ cup flaked coconut

1 cup Craisins or other sweetened dried cranberries

1 cup candied pecans, chopped

¼ cup vegetable oil

½ cup honey

1 teaspoon ground cinnamon

½ teaspoon salt

brioche french toast

This is just the right ratio of eggs to cream to yield a light golden breakfast favorite.

MAKES 4 TO 6 SERVINGS

- Beat together the eggs, half-and-half, sugar, and Grand Marnier in a shallow pie pan.

- Warm a 10-inch cast iron skillet over medium heat. Brush with vegetable oil. Dip each slice of bread quickly in the egg mixture, coating both sides. Cook until nicely browned, about 3 minutes on each side. Sprinkle with powdered sugar and serve with berry syrup.

3 large eggs
½ cup half-and-half
1 tablespoon sugar
2 tablespoons Grand Marnier (optional)
Vegetable oil
6 (1-inch-thick) slices brioche bread or egg bread
Powdered sugar, for topping
Berry syrup, for topping

chanterelle and gruyère strata with fresh thyme

Chanterelle mushrooms and eggs are a classic combination. This strata is easy to compile ahead of time. Everything is assembled two hours in advance in the buttered skillet, refrigerated, and then baked. Just pop the skillet in the preheated oven and prepare a crisp green salad to serve alongside.

. . . .

MAKES 6 SERVINGS

- Heat 2 tablespoons of the butter and the oil in a 12-inch cast iron skillet over medium heat. Add the shallots, mushrooms, and thyme and sauté, stirring occasionally, for 5 minutes. Remove from the heat, transfer the mixture from the pan, and set aside. In the warm pan, swirl the remaining 1 tablespoon butter. Layer in half of the bread, half of the chanterelle mixture, and half of the cheese and onions. Repeat the same sequence with the remainders.

- In a medium bowl beat together the half-and-half, eggs, and salt. Slowly pour the egg mixture over the top of the bread mixture. Cover and refrigerate for at least 2 hours. Remove from the refrigerator 30 minutes prior to baking.

- Preheat the oven to 350°F.

- Bake on the middle rack until golden and firm to the touch, 35 to 40 minutes. Shortly before the strata is done baking, prepare the topping. Heat the butter and olive oil in a skillet over medium heat. Add the chanterelles and sauté for 5 minutes. Remove from the heat and sprinkle with salt and pepper. Remove the strata from the oven and top with the cooked chanterelles. Serve warm.

3 tablespoons unsalted butter, divided

1 tablespoon olive oil

¼ cup minced shallots

½ pound chanterelle mushrooms, cleaned and coarsely chopped

1 tablespoon fresh thyme leaves

6 cups firm-textured white bread, cut in ¾-inch-thick cubes

2 cups grated Gruyère cheese

1 small sweet onion, quartered and thinly sliced

2½ cups half-and-half

6 large eggs

1 teaspoon kosher salt

TOPPING

2 tablespoons unsalted butter

1 tablespoon olive oil

¼ pound chanterelle mushrooms, cleaned and coarsely chopped

1 teaspoon kosher salt

Freshly ground black pepper

german apple pancake

This recipe has been in our family for many years; it's a Saturday morning favorite. Serve with well-browned little pork sausages.

. . . .

MAKES 6 SERVINGS

- Preheat the oven to 425°F.

- Melt the butter in a 12-inch cast iron skillet over medium heat. Add the apples, sugar, and cinnamon and cook, stirring several times, until apples are soft, 6 to 8 minutes. Meanwhile, put the eggs, flour, and milk in a blender and mix on medium speed just until blended, 5 to 10 seconds. Pour the batter over the apples in the skillet. Place the skillet in the oven and bake until the top puffs up and is lightly brown, 25 to 30 minutes. Serve dusted with powdered sugar and topped with whipped cream.

4 tablespoons unsalted butter

4 large Fuji apples, peeled, cored, quartered, and cut crosswise into 3/4-inch pieces

3/4 cup sugar

1/2 teaspoon ground cinnamon

4 extra-large eggs

1 cup all-purpose flour

1 cup milk

Powdered sugar, for topping

Whipped cream, for topping

small
bites

Shrimp with Smoky Tomato Pernod Sauce on Crostini
Baked Jalapeño Oysters
Skillet of Roasted Artichokes
Grilled Chicken Skewers with Spicy Peanut Sauce
Roasted Poblano and Crab Hush Puppies with Green Goddess Dipping Sauce
Imperial Stout Clams
Meatloaf Sliders on Brioche
Ginger Crab Cakes
Scallion Pancakes with Lemon Crème Fraîche Sauce, Salmon, and Sweet and Spicy Cucumbers
Sizzling Shrimp
Albacore Tuna Cakes with Lemon Parsley Sauce
Mushroom Duxelles and Goat Cheese Crostini

25

SMALL BITES OR APPETIZERS ARE AN INVITING WAY TO WELCOME friends. The Ginger Crab Cakes are full of crab, and the lemongrass is a pleasant surprise. They brown so nicely in the skillet. The Shrimp with Smoky Tomato Pernod Sauce are served on crostini, which helps to soak up all the flavors in the sauce. During the cold winter months, we use our cast iron grill pan indoors to cook appetizers such as the Grilled Chicken Skewers with Spicy Peanut Sauce. Serve the Imperial Stout Clams right from the skillet, which makes a fun presentation and keeps the clams hot. Sliders or mini-burgers are on many happy hour menus these days. Our Meatloaf Sliders on Brioche are moist and flavorful and easy to make ahead of time. ⍦ The Roasted Poblano and Crab Hush Puppies are made in a cast iron ebelskiver pan, which produces perfectly round, golden balls filled with fresh crab. A delicious way to start your evening! ⍦ Whether you're hosting a Cinco de Mayo or Super Bowl Sunday party, it's always nice to present something festive in the skillet. In the summertime, try serving a skillet full of roasted artichokes alongside a fresh crab feed. It's fun to have people over for hearty hors d'oeuvres and drinks; these small bites will add to the casual, relaxed, and easy atmosphere.

shrimp with smoky tomato pernod sauce on crostini

We love to use different spices from around the world, like Urfa biber (Urfa pepper). This moist pepper flake from Turkey is smoky and earthy, with hints of tobacco, and absolutely amazing with shrimp. The Pernod is also a favorite of ours to add to mussels and shrimp. If you pull the tails off, you can serve them over pasta. Yum!

. . . .

MAKES 25 TO 30 CROSTINI

- To prepare the crostini, set the oven to broil. Combine the garlic and olive oil. Place the baguette slices in a single layer on two baking sheets. With a pastry brush, brush the top of each slice with about 1 teaspoon of the olive oil–garlic mixture. Place under the broiler and watch carefully until the tops start to brown, 3 to 5 minutes. Remove from the oven and, using tongs, flip over the slices. Brush the other sides with the olive oil–garlic mixture and broil until light brown, another 3 to 5 minutes. Turn off oven and set crostini aside.

- To prepare the shrimp, melt 2 tablespoons of the butter in a 10- to 12-inch cast iron skillet over medium heat. Add the chopped onions and cook for 5 minutes, turn down the heat, and cook for 2 minutes more. Add the garlic and cook for another 2 minutes. Add the pureed tomatoes and Urfa biber, then stir and cook over medium-low heat for 6 to 8 minutes, until the sauce starts to thicken slightly. Drain off any excess

CROSTINI

2 cloves garlic, minced

½ cup olive oil

1 French baguette, cut at an angle into ½-inch-thick slices

SHRIMP

3 tablespoons unsalted butter, divided

1 medium onion, finely chopped

2 cloves garlic, minced

1 cup Muir Glen diced fire-roasted tomatoes, drained and pureed

1 teaspoon Urfa biber or ⅛ teaspoon crushed red pepper flakes

1 pound frozen jumbo white shrimp (21 to 25 per pound), headless, shells on

1 tablespoon Pernod (anise-flavored liqueur)

⅓ cup heavy cream

¼ teaspoon salt

⅛ teaspoon freshly ground black pepper

1 tablespoon freshly squeezed lemon juice

1 tablespoon chopped parsley, for garnish

liquid, then add the shrimp and spread out in the pan. Cook for 4 minutes, stirring gently to cook the shrimp evenly. Stir in the Pernod, cream, salt, and pepper and cook until the shrimp are pink and cooked through, about 3 minutes more. Remove from the heat, swirl in the remaining 1 tablespoon butter and lemon juice. Garnish with parsley and serve with the crostini.

baked jalapeño oysters

This is an oyster dish for those who aren't fans of raw oysters. The jalapeños add a little spice to this long-time favorite oyster recipe.

• • • • • • • • • • • • • • • • •

MAKES 8 SERVINGS

- Preheat the oven to 425°F.

- Fill a 12-inch cast iron skillet with ½ inch of coarse rock salt. Place in the oven to heat.

- Carefully shell the oysters; reserve the bottom (boat-shaped) half of each shell with the oyster liquor and the oyster. Arrange the shells on the hot rock salt. Top each oyster with a piece of bacon, 1 teaspoon cocktail sauce, 1 jalapeño slice, and 1 tablespoon cheese.

- Bake in the oven until the cheese is melted, 3 to 4 minutes. (You may need bake the oysters in two batches.) Serve immediately.

Coarse rock salt

24 oysters in their shells

6 slices bacon, cut crosswise into thick strips and cooked until crisp

½ cup cocktail sauce

4 jalapeño peppers, cut crosswise into ¼-inch-thick circles, seeds removed

1½ cups shredded sharp cheddar cheese

skillet of roasted artichokes

Springtime brings the meatiest artichokes to the market. Serve with roast chicken or bowls of fresh cracked crab. Roasting in the skillet adds more flavor than steaming.

• • • • • • • • • • • • • • • •

MAKES 4 SERVINGS

- Preheat the oven to 400°F.

- Trim the stems off the artichokes. Cut each one lengthwise into quarters. With a small paring knife, remove the fuzzy inner choke. Arrange in a 12-inch cast iron skillet. Add the lemon slices and drizzle with the olive oil. Add the water,

3 large globe artichokes
1 lemon, sliced
4 tablespoons extra-virgin olive oil
½ cup water
½ cup unsalted butter, melted, for serving

cover, and bake for 30 minutes. Remove from the oven and turn over each wedge. Drizzle with a little more oil and return to the oven, uncovered. Bake until tender, 20 to 25 minutes more. Serve with melted butter for dipping.

grilled chicken skewers with spicy peanut sauce

The cast iron grill pan makes it easy to serve these chicken skewers year-round. The peanut sauce is multiflavored—sour, sweet, salty, hot—and also a good dip for fresh vegetables. The lettuce leaves form a simple, colorful wrapper. Spread each leaf with a little peanut sauce and then place the cooked chicken on top.

• • • • • • • • • • • • • • • • •

MAKES 10 SKEWERS

- To prepare the peanut sauce, in a medium saucepan, heat the vegetable oil over medium heat. Add the shallots and sauté for 2 minutes. Add the peanut butter, brown sugar, fish sauce, and coconut milk. Cook, stirring, until the sauce is smooth and creamy. Stir in the molasses, sriracha sauce, and lime juice and remove from the heat. Serve at room temperature. The sauce can be stored in the refrigerator for several days.

- To prepare the spice rub, combine all the ingredients until well blended.

- To prepare the chicken skewers, thread the chicken strips onto the bamboo skewers. Brush with the olive oil and sprinkle lightly with the spice rub on both sides. Warm the grill pan over medium heat. When the grill is hot, brush generously with vegetable oil. Place 5 of the chicken skewers on the grill and cook for 2 to 3 minutes on each side. Serve with peanut sauce and lettuce leaves.

PEANUT SAUCE

2 tablespoons vegetable oil

3 tablespoons minced shallots

½ cup smooth peanut butter

3 tablespoons light brown sugar

2 tablespoons fish sauce

1 (13.5-ounce) can unsweetened coconut milk

2 tablespoons light molasses

2 teaspoons sriracha sauce

Freshly squeezed juice of 2 limes

SPICE RUB

1 tablespoon sweet paprika

1 tablespoon Garam Masala (see page 56)

1 teaspoon sugar

1 teaspoon sea salt

½ teaspoon ground cinnamon

⅛ teaspoon ground cloves

1 teaspoon ground coriander

CHICKEN SKEWERS

2 (8-ounce) chicken breasts, sliced at an angle into 1-by-6-inch-thick slices

10 (8-inch) bamboo skewers, soaked in water for 30 minutes

3 tablespoons extra-virgin olive oil

Vegetable oil, for grilling

Green leaf lettuce leaves

roasted poblano and crab hush puppies with green goddess dipping sauce

If you're looking for another use for your cast iron ebelskiver pan, here it is! These hush puppies are an easy-to-make, fun party appetizer. We like to serve them at a Cinco de Mayo party, but they are great anytime. Using the ebelskiver pan helps to brown them on all sides without all the oil used for traditional hush puppies. They are crispy on the outside, tender and flavorful on the inside. If you don't have time to roast a poblano pepper, you can use El Paso green Hatch chiles; use only 3 tablespoons and dry slightly on paper towels before adding. The dipping sauce is easy to whip up while the hush puppies cook.

· · · · · · · · · · · · · · · ·

MAKES 24 HUSH PUPPIES

- On an open flame of a gas burner, on a barbecue, or on a baking sheet under the broiler, roast the pepper until charred on that side. Rotate until charred all over. Transfer with tongs to a brown paper bag and close. Let the pepper steam for 5 minutes. When cool enough to handle, peel, seed, stem, and finely chop.

- Meanwhile, combine the cornmeal, flour, sugar, salt, pepper, baking powder, and baking soda and mix well. In a separate bowl combine the eggs, buttermilk, melted butter, poblano pepper, green onion, and crab (or shrimp). Fold the wet ingredients into the dry ingredients until combined. Do not overmix.

- Over medium heat, place your ebelskiver pan on the burner and allow to warm up. Add 2 teaspoons of vegetable oil to each well. Once hot, add heaping tablespoons of the batter to each well. Cook until they are golden and release easily, about 4 minutes, then flip with a skewer or fork. Cook for another 4 to 5 minutes, then plop all of them out onto a platter. Your guests will gobble them up as quickly as you make them. Continue until you have used up all the batter. Serve with Green Goddess Dipping Sauce. You can also freeze the cooked hush puppies and thaw when needed, then reheat in the ebelskiver pan.

1 poblano pepper

1½ cups yellow cornmeal, finely ground

1 cup all-purpose flour

1 tablespoon sugar

¾ teaspoon salt

½ teaspoon freshly ground black pepper

1 teaspoon baking powder

⅔ teaspoon baking soda

2 large eggs, beaten

1 cup buttermilk

¼ cup (½ stick) unsalted butter, melted

3 tablespoons finely chopped green onion

½ pound fresh crab or shrimp (if using shrimp, roughly chop)

¼ cup vegetable oil

Green Goddess Dipping Sauce (recipe follows), for serving

green goddess dipping sauce

This versatile sauce or dressing goes perfectly with seafood, and we love it on lamb sandwiches. This recipe is inspired by one of our favorite chefs, Jerry Traunfeld.

. . . .

MAKES ABOUT 2 CUPS

- Place the herbs, salt, garlic, lemon juice, anchovy paste, and mustard in a blender; puree until smooth. With the blender on low, slowly add the olive oil.

- Transfer the mixture to a medium bowl, and stir in the sour cream until well combined. Season to taste with salt and pepper.

¾ cup fresh tarragon leaves

¾ cup fresh snipped chives

¾ cup fresh Italian parsley leaves

½ teaspoon salt

1 clove garlic

¼ cup freshly squeezed lemon juice

2 tablespoons anchovy paste

1 tablespoon Dijon mustard

⅓ cup extra-virgin olive oil

¾ cup sour cream or plain yogurt

Freshly ground black pepper

imperial stout clams

Pat Donahue, executive chef at Anthony's Restaurants in the Northwest, developed this delicious recipe for manila clams. Serve as an appetizer with grilled bread for dipping in the sauce.

. . . .

MAKES 2 TO 4 SERVINGS

- Wash the clams well and discard any that are broken. In a 10-inch cast iron skillet, melt the butter. Add the bell pepper and onion and sauté just until they start to soften. Sprinkle with the flour and stir to mix into the butter. Add the black pepper, beer, and clam juice. Add the clams, cover, and steam until all the clams are open, 5 to 7 minutes. Serve with a nice loaf of sliced crusty bread.

1 pound manila clams

¼ cup (½ stick) unsalted butter

½ red bell pepper, cut into strips ¼ inch by 2 inches

¼ sweet yellow onion, cut into crescent strips

1 tablespoon all-purpose flour

¼ teaspoon freshly ground black pepper

¼ cup dark beer

½ cup clam juice

meatloaf sliders on brioche

These perfectly moist mini-sandwiches are also great for lunch, hot or cold. Serve them up on a platter with your favorite beer or root beer. You'll find pickled jalapeños in the Mexican or ethnic foods section of most grocery stores.

. . . .

MAKES 10 TO 12 SERVINGS

- Preheat the oven to 350°F.

- To prepare the meatloaf, combine the beef and pork in a large bowl. In a medium bowl mix together the eggs, milk, and Worcestershire sauce, then add to the meat along with the jalapeño, onion, bread crumbs, salt, pepper, and chili sauce. Mix well. On a cutting board, divide the meat mixture in half and form into two 3-by-8-inch loaves. Place in a 10-inch cast iron skillet. Bake until a meat thermometer reads 155°F, 35 to 40 minutes. Allow the meatloaf to cool for 10 minutes (or refrigerate) before cutting into 1-inch-thick slices.

- To prepare the sauce, combine the ketchup, mayonnaise, and relish in a small bowl and set aside.

- To assemble, toast the brioche. Spread 1 tablespoon of the sauce on each side of the buns. For each sandwich, use 1 slice of meatloaf and 2 or 3 pickled jalapeños, depending on how much heat you like. Top with a few slices of onion and the other bun half. Serve on a platter.

MEATLOAF

1 pound ground beef

½ pound ground pork

2 large eggs

½ cup milk

1 tablespoon Worcestershire sauce

1 tablespoon finely diced jalapeño

½ cup finely diced yellow onion

1 cup soft fresh bread crumbs

1 teaspoon salt

¼ teaspoon freshly ground black pepper

½ cup Heinz or other chili sauce

SAUCE

½ cup ketchup

1 cup mayonnaise

¼ cup sweet pickle relish

. . . .

10 to 12 small brioche or slider buns

¼ cup pickled jalapeños (optional)

½ sweet yellow onion, thinly sliced

ginger crab cakes

The ginger and lemon gives these crab cakes a refreshing taste, complementing the crab without overpowering. You can make small 2-inch cakes at parties as an appetizer or larger 4-inch cakes as a main course. We love to serve these with a Japanese curry sauce called *katsu*; look for it in the Asian and ethnic aisle of your supermarket.

● ● ● ● ● ● ● ● ● ● ● ● ● ● ● ●

MAKES 12 CAKES

- Preheat the oven to 225°F.

- In a large bowl, combine all the ingredients expect the crab and vegetable oil. Fold in the crabmeat. Form into cakes about 1 inch thick. If the mixture will not form a firm cake, mix in 2 tablespoons more mayonnaise.

- Cover a baking sheet with layers of paper towels to drain the cakes. Heat 2 tablespoons of the oil in a 10- or 12-inch cast iron skillet over medium-high heat. Gently place 6 cakes in the pan and cook until golden, about 5 minutes on each side, turning the cakes with a spatula. If the pan gets too hot, turn down the heat to medium-low. Transfer the cakes to the paper towel-lined baking sheet and place in the oven to keep warm. Add 2 more tablespoons oil to the pan and cook the remaining cakes.

½ cup mayonnaise

1 large egg, beaten

2 teaspoons peeled, finely grated fresh ginger or ginger paste

¼ cup finely chopped red bell pepper

1 tablespoon finely chopped shallot

1 tablespoon Worcestershire

1 teaspoon lemongrass paste or lemon zest

1 tablespoon freshly squeezed lemon juice

2 teaspoons prepared Dijon mustard

¼ cup thinly sliced green onions

¼ teaspoon salt

¼ teaspoon freshly ground black pepper

1 cup finely crushed saltine crackers

½ pound fresh Dungeness crabmeat

4 tablespoons vegetable oil, for frying

scallion pancakes with lemon crème fraîche sauce, salmon, and sweet and spicy cucumbers

Scallion pancakes are a great appetizer on their own or as a side served alongside a dish such as moo-shu pork. Once you get into the swing of things, you'll realize how easy these pancakes are to make. You can prepare a batch or two and freeze them for later use, but there is nothing better than eating these hot from the skillet. Be sure to start marinating the cucumbers the day before so the flavor has time to develop.

MAKES 8 SERVINGS

- To prepare the cucumbers, place them in a small bowl and toss with 2 teaspoons of the salt so the slices release excess moisture. After about 5 minutes, lightly rinse the cucumbers, then pat dry with paper towels.

- In a medium nonreactive bowl, combine the remaining salt, vinegar, sugar, water, and ginger. Add the cucumbers to the marinade and gently toss. Cover with plastic wrap and refrigerate for 2 to 3 hours or overnight. The flavor gets better after the second day. They will keep for 5 to 7 days.

- To prepare the crème fraîche sauce, in a small bowl, combine the crème fraîche, lemon juice and zest, and salt. Stir until smooth.

- To prepare the pancakes, in a large bowl, combine the flour and salt. Add the hot water and mix well with a wooden spoon until incorporated. Bring the dough together and knead for a few minutes; if the dough is still sticky, add a little more flour. Place the dough in a lightly oiled bowl, cover with a damp towel, and let rest for 30 minutes.

SWEET AND SPICY CUCUMBERS

1 English cucumber, cut into ¼-inch-thick slices

3 teaspoons salt, divided

¼ cup rice wine vinegar

2 tablespoons sugar

⅔ cup water

3 thin slices unpeeled ginger

LEMON CRÈME FRAÎCHE SAUCE

1½ cups crème fraîche, or sour cream thinned with ¼ cup heavy cream

2 tablespoons freshly squeezed lemon juice

1 teaspoon lemon zest

½ teaspoon salt

SCALLION PANCAKES

2 cups all-purpose flour

¼ teaspoon salt

⅔ cup hot water

4 teaspoons sesame oil or vegetable oil, divided

1 teaspoon salt, divided

½ cup finely chopped green onions, divided

¼ cup vegetable oil, for cooking

1 cup smoked salmon, broken into 1-inch pieces

Pickled ginger, for garnish (optional)

- Preheat the oven to 225°F.

- Turn out the dough onto a lightly floured surface. Cut into 4 equal pieces. Place a moist towel over the 3 pieces you are not working with. Roll out each piece into a 6-inch rectangle about ¼ inch thick. Rub the top lightly with 1 teaspoon sesame oil, then sprinkle with ¼ teaspoon salt and 2 tablespoons green onions. Starting at one end, roll up the dough like a cinnamon roll. Starting at one end of the rolled log, coil it up lengthwise like a snail shell. Set aside and cover with a moist towel. Repeat with the other 3 pieces of dough.

- On a lightly floured surface, using a rolling pin, carefully roll out each dough coil to form a ¼- to ½-inch-thick pancake. Heat 1 tablespoon of the vegetable oil in a 10- or 12-inch cast iron skillet over medium-high heat. When hot, add a pancake and cook until golden brown, 2 to 3 minutes. Flip and cook for another 2 to 3 minutes. Remove from the pan and cut into 8 wedges. Transfer to a baking sheet in the preheated oven to keep warm. Repeat with the rest of the dough.

- To serve, assemble the pancakes by placing 2 teaspoons crème fraîche sauce, a piece of salmon, 1 or 2 cucumber slices, and a slice of pickled ginger atop each pancake wedge.

sizzling shrimp

Always keep a bag of frozen shrimp in your freezer, available to serve as a last-minute appetizer. They don't take long to thaw, and cooking them takes only 5 minutes. Besar is a spice blend from the United Arab Emirates–it is a combination of cinnamon, Tellicherry pepper, cumin, coriander, fennel, turmeric, and chili flakes; it pairs well with just about any savory dish. These spicy-sweet cocktail shrimp disappear quickly. Serve directly from the skillet.

● ● ● ● ● ● ● ● ● ● ● ● ● ● ● ●

MAKES 4 SERVINGS

- Melt the butter in a 10-inch cast iron skillet over medium heat. Add the smoked paprika, brown sugar, oregano, and sea salt. Stir until well blended, 2 to 3 minutes. Add the shrimp and turn several times with a spatula. Add the lemon zest and besar and cook until shrimp are pink all the way through, about 5 minutes. Add the lemon juice and sriracha sauce, and serve warm in the skillet.

4 tablespoons unsalted butter

2 teaspoons smoked paprika

2 tablespoons brown sugar

½ teaspoon dried oregano

1 teaspoon sea salt

1 pound shrimp (16 to 20 per pound), shelled, well drained, and patted dry

1 teaspoon freshly grated lemon zest

1 teaspoon besar spice blend (optional)

1 tablespoon freshly squeezed lemon juice

Dash of sriracha or other hot sauce

albacore tuna cakes with lemon parsley sauce

These are a great and inexpensive alternative to crab cakes. Dolphin-safe, albacore white tuna packed in water is our favorite. You can also add 1 tablespoon capers for a nice pickled flavor. Pass around a basket of lightly grilled rustic bread.

. . . .

MAKES 10 CAKES

- Preheat the oven to 250°F.

- To prepare the cakes, in a large bowl, crumble the tuna into small pieces. Add the mayonnaise and mix. Add the egg, lemon zest and juice, saltines, pickle, paprika, cumin, mustard, Worcestershire, goat cheese, and pepper, and mix well. Form ¼ cup of the mixture into a ball, then flatten into a disk or cake and place on a baking sheet.

- Heat 2 tablespoons of the vegetable oil in a 10- or 12-inch cast iron skillet over medium-high heat. Cover a cooling rack with layers of paper towels to drain the cakes. Add 5 cakes, without crowding, to the pan.

- Cook until golden brown, about 5 minutes on each side, turning the cakes with a spatula. If the pan starts to smoke, turn the heat down to medium. Transfer from the pan to the paper towels, then place on a baking sheet and put in the oven to keep warm. Add the remaining 2 tablespoons oil to the pan and cook the rest of the cakes. Dress the greens and arrange on individual plates. Place one or two cakes on each bed of greens.

- To prepare the sauce, combine the mayonnaise or aioli with the parsley and paprika until smooth. Place 1 teaspoon of the aioli on each cake and serve.

CAKES

2 (7-ounce) cans albacore tuna, drained

¼ cup mayonnaise

1 large egg, beaten

1 teaspoon freshly grated lemon zest

1 tablespoon freshly squeezed lemon juice

8 saltine squares, crushed

1 dill pickle, finely chopped

½ teaspoon smoked paprika or regular paprika

½ teaspoon ground cumin

2 teaspoons prepared Dijon mustard

1 tablespoon Worcestershire sauce

¼ cup goat cheese, crumbled

¼ teaspoon freshly ground black pepper

4 tablespoons vegetable oil, for cooking

Salad greens, for serving

Light citrus dressing, for serving

LEMON PARSLEY SAUCE

4 tablespoons mayonnaise or Lemon Aioli (recipe follows)

1 tablespoon chopped parsley

½ teaspoon smoked paprika

lemon aioli

When making aioli, be careful not to over-whisk it or the mixture will separate. However, if this happens, you can beat another egg yolk in a separate bowl, pour in the separated aioli, and carefully whisk to combine.

. . . .

MAKES ABOUT 1 CUP

2 cloves garlic

¼ teaspoon salt

1 egg yolk

1 teaspoon water

1 tablespoon freshly squeezed lemon juice

1¼ cups extra-virgin olive oil

- Using a mortar and pestle, crush the garlic and salt into a paste. Transfer to a medium-sized glass or other nonreactive bowl. Add the egg yolk and whisk well. Stir in the water and lemon juice. Gradually whisk in the olive oil 1 tablespoon at a time, stirring after each addition, until you have incorporated about ⅔ cup. Whisking constantly, drizzle the remaining olive oil into the aioli in a very slow stream. If the aioli is too thick, add another teaspoon of water and stir to combine. Taste for seasoning and adjust if necessary.

mushroom duxelles and goat cheese crostini

We have always loved the simplicity of sautéed mushrooms on toast. The goat cheese with the mushrooms is so delicious, these crostini disappear quickly!

. . . .

MAKES 35 CROSTINI

- Preheat the broiler.

- Place the baguette slices in a single layer on two baking sheets. Combine the garlic and the olive oil. With a pastry brush, brush the baguette slices with about 1 teaspoon of the mixture. Place under the broiler and watch carefully until the tops start to brown, 3 to 5 minutes. When light brown, remove from the oven with tongs. Flip over the slices and brush the other side with the olive oil-garlic mixture and broil until light brown, another 3 to 5 minutes. Remove, turn off oven, and set aside.

- To prepare the duxelles, place the mushrooms on several layers of paper towels. Sprinkle with the salt and let sit for 3 minutes.

CROSTINI

1 baguette, sliced at an angle or diagonally, ½-inch thick

2 cloves garlic, minced

½ cup olive oil, divided

DUXELLES

¾ pound fresh cremini mushrooms or assorted mushrooms such as chanterelles, cremini, hedgehog, or morels, cleaned and finely chopped

½ teaspoon salt

4 tablespoons unsalted butter

4 tablespoons finely chopped shallots

1 teaspoon finely chopped fresh parsley

1 teaspoon finely chopped fresh chives

¼ teaspoon salt

Freshly ground black pepper

. . . .

¼ cup fresh goat cheese

Salt and freshly ground black pepper

- Place another layer of paper towels on top. Press down to squeeze out any excess juices from the mushrooms. In a 10- or 12-inch cast iron skillet, heat the butter over medium heat. Once hot, add the shallots and cook, stirring constantly, until soft, about 2 minutes. Add the mushrooms and cook until all the moisture has evaporated and they begin to brown, about 10 minutes. Transfer to a bowl and stir in the parsley, chives, salt, and pepper.

- Arrange the crostini on a platter and place 1 tablespoon duxelles on top of each. Crumble the goat cheese over the tops, sprinkle lightly with salt and pepper, and serve.

main dishes

47

SET THE STAGE WITH A DELICIOUS ENTRÉE. SEARING MEATS AND FISH, TEA SMOKING, and cooking crab wok-style are some of the cooking techniques you can do successfully in the skillet. We've found that many of the wonderful spices and spice blends we're cooking with can be found at the local grocery store or ordered online. Stock your pantry with a range of spices, and when you want to cook some of these recipes you'll have the ingredients already on hand. ⎟ We are fortunate to live near a large Asian grocery store, Uwajimaya. When you walk in, you can easily be overwhelmed by aisles lined with sauces, noodles, fermented this, and pickled that. Just take your time; start small and add slowly to your shelves some of our favorites, such as miso, furikake (Asian seasoning), black rice wine vinegar, sriracha, fish sauce, tamarind paste, oyster sauce, hoisin sauce, and curry pastes. We are always bringing home something new to try. Ginger Chow Fun Noodles satisfy our craving for Asian flavors: hot, sour, salty, and sweet are all components in the sauce. Smoky Smothered Chicken makes a good choice for a family Sunday supper. Seared Salmon with Roasted Tomato, Olive, and Bacon Relish is a candidate for a company dinner when fresh salmon is in season. ⎟ Heat up your cast iron skillet with big flavors and enjoy!

Cast iron's dry, even heat is a great choice for the following cooking methods.

Braising is ideal for the tough muscle cuts of meat, such as chuck roast, short ribs, and shanks. It is important to brown the meat first and then add the amount of liquid specified in the recipe. The browning and caramelizing of the outside of the meat is best done in a heated cast iron pan with a little oil or butter. When you try to brown or caramelize in a nonstick skillet, excess moisture develops, which prevents browning and tightens and toughens the meat. Ground beef actually browns and crisps in cast iron, rather that stewing and becoming flavorless and grey as it does in other types of pans.

Pan-searing in a cast iron skillet creates a flavorful, brown crust on tender cuts of meat such as pork chops or tenderloin, steaks, and fish fillets. To pan-sear, first season the meat or fish with the desired spice rub or seasoning. Heat the skillet over medium-high heat, add a little olive oil, and sear both sides of the meat or fish in the skillet. Then place the skillet with the meat or fish in a preheated 375°F oven and finish cooking according to the recipe. When pan-searing fish, scallops, skinless chicken, or pork, wait until a golden crust forms. If the flesh sticks to the pan, it's not ready to be turned over yet.

Roasting in the cast iron skillet creates a dry, even heat like a hearth oven. Roasting vegetables in the skillet, tossed with a little oil, browns and caramelizes them perfectly.

Sautéing is a gentle approach to cooking using medium heat. We like to use a little oil and butter combined to achieve a nice browning.

Stir-frying in a cast iron skillet works best over medium-high heat. Be sure to have all your ingredients chopped, sliced, and diced, ready to add to the hot skillet. Heat the pan over medium-high heat, then add the oil, swirling it around to distribute evenly. You want to keep your ingredients moving around in the pan continuously, using a wooden spatula or tongs.

herb-crusted lamb tenderloins with cilantro-mint chutney

This lamb has a wonderful hint of citrus from the sumac in the rub, and is crispy on the outside, tender on the inside. The tenderloin is delicious served with the chutney for dinner, and it makes a great sandwich the following day.

Note: Ask the butcher for the tenderloin, and if they come as two tenderloins tied together, have the butcher untie them and trim off the fat. If they have a small tenderloin attached, remove and use in the same manner as described here, cooking 3 to 4 minutes on each side.

· · · · · · · · · · · · · · · · ·

MAKES 4 SERVINGS

- Preheat the oven to 400°F.

- Put the parsley, thyme, and chives in a glass baking dish.

- Rub the tenderloins with 2 tablespoons of the olive oil, then with the Syrian Zahtar Rub. Sprinkle with salt and pepper, then roll them in the herb mixture until well coated.

- Heat a 10- to 12-inch cast iron skillet over medium-high heat. When hot, add the tenderloins and cook for 5 minutes. Turn over for 30 seconds to sear the other side, then transfer to the hot oven for 5 minutes more. Line a plate with enough aluminum foil to wrap around the tenderloins. Transfer them from the oven to the foil-lined plate, wrap loosely, and let rest for 5 minutes. Slice at an angle and serve with rice, with Cilantro-Mint Chutney spooned over.

¼ cup fresh chervil or Italian parsley

1 tablespoon fresh thyme leaves

2 tablespoons finely chopped fresh chives

2 lamb tenderloins, fat removed

2 tablespoons olive oil, divided

3 tablespoons Syrian Zahtar Rub (recipe follows)

1 teaspoon kosher salt

¼ teaspoon freshly ground black pepper

Jasmine rice, for serving

Cilantro-Mint Chutney (recipe follows), for serving

syrian zahtar rub

MAKES ¼ CUP

- Toast the coriander, cumin, and fennel seeds in a small cast iron skillet over medium heat. Swirl in the pan until toasted and fragrant, about 3 minutes. Remove from the heat and cool slightly. Add the toasted seeds and all the other ingredients to a spice grinder and grind until well blended.

1 teaspoon coriander seeds

1 teaspoon cumin seeds

1 teaspoon fennel seeds

½ teaspoon toasted sesame seeds (optional)

¼ cup ground sumac

2 teaspoons dried thyme leaves

½ teaspoon paprika

¼ teaspoon salt

cilantro-mint chutney

Used in Indian cuisine, this is a delicious sauce served with seafood or on sandwiches. Some recipes include nuts or coconut; our features toasted cumin seeds.

. . . .

MAKES 1½ CUPS

- Toast the cumin seeds in a small cast iron skillet over medium heat. Swirl in the pan until toasted and fragrant, about 3 minutes. Remove from the heat and grind in a spice grinder. Add the ground cumin and all the other ingredients to a blender and blend to a paste. Taste for salt. Transfer from the blender to a serving bowl. If the chutney is too thick, stir in a little water.

½ teaspoon cumin seeds or ¼ teaspoon ground cumin

2 teaspoons Dijon mustard

1 cup fresh cilantro leaves

¼ cup chopped fresh mint leaves

1 clove garlic

1 teaspoon sliced fresh ginger

½ jalapeño, seeded and finely diced

2 tablespoons unsweetened shredded coconut

2 tablespoons raisins, soaked in hot water for 10 minutes, then drained

1 tablespoon freshly squeezed lime juice

½ cup plain yogurt

1 tablespoon olive oil

¼ teaspoon salt

beef brisket with chili cider sauce on ciabatta rolls

Brisket has always been one of our favorite cuts of beef for slow-cooking. With this method, the onions caramelize and the meat gets tender, then it's all bundled into ciabatta buns with cheddar mayonnaise, pickled jalapeños, and crispy romaine. The heat from the jalapeños is a pleasant surprise.

. . . .

MAKES 8 SERVINGS

- Preheat the oven to 325°F.

- To prepare the brisket, flour the meat lightly and season with the salt. Heat the oil in a 12-inch cast iron skillet over medium heat. Brown the meat on both sides. Mix the chili sauce with the cider and pour over the brisket. Scatter the onions over the top. Place a piece of parchment paper over the meat. Cover and bake for 2 hours. Uncover and bake for 1 hour more. Remove from the oven and let rest for 10 minutes before slicing or shredding.

- To prepare the Cheddar-Mayo Spread, in a small bowl, blend together the mayonnaise, cheddar, horseradish, and mustard.

- To assemble the sandwiches, spread 3 tablespoons of the spread on one side of each ciabatta roll. Place 4 to 5 jalapeño slices on top of the spread. Add a romaine leaf, then add 4 slices of brisket and top with onions. Close and serve.

One 4- to 5-pound beef brisket

¼ cup all-purpose flour

½ teaspoon salt

2 tablespoons vegetable oil

1 cup chili sauce

12 ounces fresh apple cider

1 sweet yellow onion, cut in half and sliced into crescents

CHEDDAR-MAYO SPREAD

¾ cup mayonnaise

1 cup grated cheddar

1 tablespoon prepared horseradish

1 teaspoon Dijon mustard

. . . .

8 ciabatta rolls

½ cup pickled jalapeño slices

8 romaine lettuce leaves

butter-poached chicken in garam masala sauce with jasmine rice

This is a fresh, light chicken dinner with lovely coconut-scented jasmine rice. The chicken is very moist and the sauce has great flavor. Serve with a fresh fruit salad.

. . . .

MAKES 4 SERVINGS

- To prepare the rice, put the rice and water in a 2-quart pot over medium-high heat and bring to a boil. Turn the heat down to low, cover, and simmer until all the liquid is absorbed and the rice is tender, 18 to 20 minutes. Remove from the heat and let sit for 5 minutes. Pour the coconut milk over the rice and fluff with a fork. Set aside.

- To prepare the poached chicken, sprinkle the chicken pieces with the flour. Melt the butter in a 12-inch cast iron skillet over medium heat and sauté the chicken pieces for 5 minutes, turning once. Transfer the chicken to a plate and set aside.

- To prepare the sauce, in the same skillet used to poach the chicken, over medium heat, add the butter, jalapeño, ginger, and onions. Sprinkle in the garam masala, coriander, and paprika and cook for 5 minutes, stirring often. Add the chicken broth and tomatoes, and simmer for 10 minutes. Add the coconut milk and simmer for 5 minutes. Add the chicken, stir gently, and cook uncovered, for 10 minutes, or until heated through. Season with salt and pepper to taste.

- To serve, spoon the chicken onto a bed of the jasmine rice and garnish with the green onions and cilantro.

COCONUT-SCENTED JASMINE RICE

2 cups jasmine rice, well rinsed

2½ cups water

¼ cup coconut milk

POACHED CHICKEN

2 tablespoons all-purpose flour

4 boneless, skinless chicken breasts, each cut into 4 pieces

4 tablespoons unsalted butter

GARAM MASALA SAUCE

4 tablespoons unsalted butter

1 tablespoon chopped jalapeño pepper, seeded

1 tablespoon minced fresh ginger

1½ cups chopped yellow onion

2 teaspoons Garam Masala (recipe follows)

1 teaspoon ground coriander

2 teaspoons sweet paprika

1 cup chicken broth

1 (14.5-ounce) can diced tomatoes, drained

1 cup coconut milk

Salt and freshly ground black pepper

½ cup chopped green onions, for garnish

½ cup chopped fresh cilantro, for garnish

Fruit Salad with Poppy Seed Dressing (recipe follows)

garam masala

Garam masala is popular in Indian dishes as well as other South Asian cuisines. The word "garam" refers to the intensity of the spice, not the heat of the spice. It is very versatile; we like to use it sprinkled on meats as a rub or as a seasoning for vegetables. It is available at grocery stores in the spice section, or you can make your own using our recipe. We like to toast and grind the spices as we use them. Toasting the spices lightly in the cast iron skillet brings out the rich flavor. After toasting, store in spice jars.

MAKES ⅓ CUP

- In a cast iron skillet over medium heat, toast the coriander, cumin, peppercorns, mustard seeds, cloves, and cinnamon stick for 2 to 3 minutes, stirring the spices around with a wooden spoon. Once toasted and aromatic, transfer to a glass measuring cup and add the remaining spices. Then pour into a coffee/spice grinder or a mortar and pestle and grind to a powder. Spread out to cool. When cooled, place in airtight glass spice jars, label, and date; it will keep for 6 to 8 months.

2 tablespoons coriander seeds

2 tablespoon cumin seeds

1 tablespoon whole black peppercorns

2 teaspoons mustard seeds

¼ teaspoon whole cloves

1-inch stick cassia or cinnamon, broken up, or 1 teaspoon ground cinnamon

1 teaspoon ground cardamom

1 teaspoon ground ginger

½ teaspoon freshly grated nutmeg

2 bay leaves

fruit salad with poppy seed dressing

MAKES 4 TO 6 SERVINGS

- To make the dressing, combine the sugar, salt, mustard, and vinegar in a mixing bowl. Add the onion and mix well. Slowly whisk in the oil until fully incorporated. Stir in the poppy seeds. Mix well before using.

- To make the fruit salad, toss the bananas, pineapple, papaya, and kiwi in a large bowl. Stir in ½ to ¾ cup of the dressing to lightly coat the fruit. Serve immediately. Store any leftover dressing in the refrigerator for up to 1 week; use on spinach salad or coleslaw.

POPPY SEED DRESSING

½ cup plus 3 tablespoons sugar

½ teaspoon salt

¾ teaspoon dry mustard

⅓ cup white vinegar

1½ tablespoons grated sweet onion

½ cup vegetable oil

1 tablespoon poppy seeds

FRUIT SALAD

2 bananas, sliced

2 cups fresh pineapple chunks

1 papaya, cut into 1-inch pieces

3 kiwifruits, peeled and diced

easy cast iron skillet cassoulet

A 12-inch cast iron skillet serves well as a baking pan for this hearty winter casserole. Using canned beans and smoked meats, it's easy to assemble: everything comes from your pantry except the meats. Serve with a crusty baguette and a green salad for a simple, satisfying supper. If there is any left over, reheat it and serve for lunch the next day. We made this one day after our cupboard was overstocked with canned beans and diced tomatoes. It turned out so well, we've made it for company ever since as a simple Sunday supper.

. . . .

MAKES 6 SERVINGS

- In a 12-inch cast iron skillet, sauté the bacon until crisp. Transfer to a paper towel to drain. Add the sausage to the skillet and brown lightly. Remove from the pan and reserve.

- Add the olive oil, onions, and garlic to the pan and sauté for 5 minutes. Stir in the rosemary, thyme, and red pepper flakes. Add the beans, tomatoes, broth, tomato paste, bacon, sausage, and smoked pork. Simmer over low heat for 25 minutes. Meanwhile, melt the butter in a separate skillet. Add the bread crumbs and stir to coat evenly.

- Preheat the oven to 350°F.

- Spread the buttered crumbs over the beans and meat and bake for 30 minutes. When the cassoulet is bubbling and the crumbs are nicely browned, it's ready to serve.

4 slices bacon, diced

1 pound smoked, fully cooked sausage, cut crosswise into ¾-inch slices

4 tablespoons olive oil

1 cup chopped yellow onion

4 cloves garlic, chopped

1 tablespoon chopped fresh rosemary

1 teaspoon fresh thyme leaves

½ teaspoon red pepper flakes

3 (15-ounce) cans Great Northern beans, rinsed and drained

1 (15-ounce) can diced tomatoes with juice

¾ cup chicken broth

3 tablespoons tomato paste

4 smoked pork chops, cut in half, bone removed

6 tablespoons unsalted butter

4 cups coarse fresh bread crumbs

fideus de gambas

While visiting relatives in Barcelona, we had the opportunity to eat *fideus*, a variation of paella using broken noodles instead of rice. Thin noodles are broken into three-inch lengths, then browned in olive oil before any liquid is added. This is a delicious foundation for seafood or vegetables. We especially like it with steamed clams or mussels on the side.

• • • • • • • • • • • • • • • • • • •

MAKES 6 SERVINGS

- Preheat the oven to 350°F.

- Break the noodles into 2- to 3-inch pieces. Heat the oil in a 10- to 12-inch cast iron skillet. Add the noodles and cook, stirring often, until they start to brown, 6 to 8 minutes.

- With a spoon, make a hole in the center and add the garlic. Cook for 2 minutes, then add the onion, paprika, tomatoes and their juice, and saffron. Add the chicken broth, and bring to a boil, stirring often. Transfer to the oven and bake, uncovered, for 30 minutes. Stir in the prawns and bake for 5 minutes more. Serve hot or warm.

½ pound dry, uncooked angel hair pasta

⅓ cup olive oil

3 cloves garlic, minced

¾ cup chopped yellow onion

½ teaspoon smoked paprika

1 (14.5-ounce) can chopped tomatoes with juice

½ teaspoon saffron threads

4 cups chicken broth

½ pound medium prawns, deveined and peeled

skillet-roasted mussels

These mussels are simple and delicious! Serve as an appetizer with a loaf of your favorite crusty bread. The Pernod is optional but adds a nice, unexpected flavor.

Note: If any of the mussels are open when you bring them home and do not close when pinched, or if the shells are broken, discard them.

· · · · · · · · · · · · · · · · · ·

MAKES 4 SERVINGS

- In a 10- to 12-inch cast iron skillet over medium-high heat, combine the white wine, Pernod, butter, leeks, and red pepper flakes and bring to a boil. Turn the heat down to medium and add the mussels.

- Cover the pan and cook for 6 minutes. Remove the lid and add the peppers. Drizzle the melted butter over the mussels. Replace the lid and cook until the mussels are open and plump, about 3 minutes.

- Sprinkle with the parsley, and serve right from the skillet with sliced crusty bread.

1 cup white wine

3 tablespoons Pernod (anise-flavored liqueur), optional

2 tablespoons unsalted butter

1 leek, white part only, trimmed, well rinsed, and coarsely chopped

¼ teaspoon red pepper flakes

2 pounds fresh mussels, debearded just before cooking

¼ cup diced red bell pepper

¼ cup diced yellow bell pepper

4 tablespoons unsalted butter, melted

3 tablespoons chopped parsley, for garnish

clams with sausage, ham, and spices

This recipe hails from Portugal, where they cook the clams in a *cataplana*–a clamshell-shaped metal or copper casserole. But not everyone owns a *cataplana*, and we've found that the cast iron skillet is a perfect substitute. This is a very flavorful dish; we love the heat and saltiness you get from the sausage and the ham. When serving this dish as an entrée, serve the clams over brown or Spanish rice, or serve with a fennel salad and a loaf of crusty French bread.

. . . .

MAKES 4 SERVINGS AS A MAIN DISH OR 6 TO 8 SERVINGS AS AN APPETIZER

½ pound linguica sausage or chorizo or other smoked sausage

¼ cup olive oil

2 medium onions, halved and thinly sliced

1 teaspoon paprika

¼ teaspoon crushed hot red pepper flakes

Freshly ground black pepper

3 ounces serrano ham, prosciutto, or other lean smoked ham, sliced into ½-inch pieces

2 medium tomatoes, peeled, seeded, and coarsely chopped

¼ cup plus 2 tablespoons finely chopped flat-leaf parsley

½ cup dry white wine

1 clove garlic, finely chopped

2 small bay leaves, broken into pieces

1½ pounds small clams, washed and scrubbed

2 tablespoons freshly squeezed lemon juice or ½ lemon

- Bring a pan of water to a boil. With a small, sharp knife, remove the casing from the sausages. Crumble the meat coarsely and drop it into a sieve. Plunge the sieve into the boiling water and boil briskly for 1 minute. Then spread the sausage meat out on layers of paper towels to drain.

- In a 10- or 12-inch cast iron skillet, heat the olive oil over medium heat. Once hot, add the onions and stir frequently. Cook until they are soft and transparent but not brown, about 5 minutes. Add the paprika, red pepper flakes, and a generous grinding of black pepper. Cook for a minute or two. Add the sausage meat, ham, tomatoes, ¼ cup of the parsley, wine, garlic, and bay leaves, raise the heat, and bring to a boil. Stirring constantly, cook briskly until most of the liquid has cooked off. Arrange the clams over the meat and tomato mixture. Cover with a lid or foil and cook over medium heat until all the clams open, about 10 minutes. Discard any that remain closed. Squeeze the lemon juice over the clams and sprinkle with the remaining parsley.

- To serve, transfer the clams to warm soup bowls and ladle sauce over them.

fish tacos with avocado tomatillo crema

There are several elements involved in putting this dish together, but once you have everything ready to go, you'll be amazed at how quickly these tacos cook up–and disappear! If you ever find you don't have the time to make the pico de gallo, just buy your favorite brand of fresh salsa.

. . . .

MAKES 8 TO 10 TACOS

- Preheat the oven to 200°F.

- Wrap the tortillas together in a moist paper towel, then wrap in foil. Place in the oven to warm through.

- To prepare the avocado tomatillo cream, put the salsa verde, cilantro, avocado, garlic, jalapeño, and lime juice in a blender and blend well. Pour into a bowl and whisk in the crema. Refrigerate.

- To prepare the pico de gallo, combine all the ingredients and let rest for 30 minutes while you prepare the fish.

- To prepare the rub, combine all the ingredients in a small bowl.

- To prepare the fish, rub each piece with 2 teaspoons olive oil. Then sprinkle 2 teaspoons of the rub on each side of the fish.

- Heat a 10- to 12-inch cast iron skillet over medium heat. Swirl in 2 tablespoons olive oil until hot. Add 3 pieces of fish and cook for 3 minutes on each side. Remove to a warm plate. Add 2 more tablespoons olive oil to the skillet, heat, and cook the remaining fish. Cut each fish fillet in half to make 12 pieces of fish.

12 small flour tortillas

AVOCADO TOMATILLO CREMA

½ cup salsa verde, preferably Embasa or Herdez

1 cup coarsely chopped fresh cilantro

1 avocado

1 clove garlic

½ jalapeño, seeded

Juice of ½ lime

¾ cup Mexican crema or sour cream

PICO DE GALLO

2 cups (about 4) diced tomatoes

1 clove garlic, minced

¼ cup diced white onion

Juice of 1 lime

¼ cup chopped fresh cilantro

2 jalapeños, stems and seeds removed, diced

½ tablespoon olive oil

Salt

RUB

Zest of 2 lemons

2 teaspoons chili powder

2 teaspoons fine herb blend or herbes de Provence

2 teaspoons salt

¼ teaspoon freshly ground black pepper

. . . .

- To assemble, place a warmed tortilla on each plate. Add 2 tablespoons avocado tomatillo crema, a handful of shredded lettuce, and a piece of fish. Spoon a portion of pico de gallo over the top and serve with lime wedges.

2½ pounds cod or rockfish fillets, skin removed, cut into 6 pieces

4 tablespoons olive oil

6 cups shredded iceberg lettuce

2 limes, quartered, for garnish

ginger chow fun noodles

Our good friends Larry and Sally Brown shared this recipe with us. They spend their vacations in Hawaii and enjoy new food experiences. This is one of their favorite dishes from the islands. Assemble all the ingredients ahead of cooking and then quickly stir-fry.

. . . .

MAKES 4 SERVINGS

- Bring a large pot of water to a boil. Briefly blanch the carrots, then the beans, and reserve. Cook the noodles in the same water and drain well.

- Heat a 12-inch cast iron skillet over medium heat. Add the oil and swirl to coat the pan evenly. Stir in the garlic and ginger. Add the pork, breaking it up into small pieces. When browned, add the soy sauce. Stir in the reserved carrots and green beans. Add the noodles and the sesame oil, oyster sauce, and hoisin sauce. Serve in individual bowls topped with bean sprouts and green onions.

1 cup julienned carrots

1 cup green beans, sliced diagonally into 2-inch pieces

12 ounces Chow Fun noodles or fresh egg fettuccini

2 tablespoons vegetable oil

2 cloves garlic, minced

1 tablespoon minced fresh ginger

½ pound fresh ground pork

3 tablespoons soy sauce

2 tablespoons sesame oil

1 tablespoon oyster sauce

1 tablespoon hoisin sauce

1 cup fresh bean sprouts, for topping

¼ cup chopped green onion, for topping

chicken and cashew red curry

The cast iron skillet works almost as well as a wok for stir-frying. The key to a good stir-fry is to cook it quickly over high heat. It's important to have all your ingredients ready before you start cooking. Adding the sugar snap peas in the last few minutes adds a tender-crunchy green element. Serve with white or brown rice.

. . . .

MAKES 4 SERVINGS

- To prepare the sauce, in a medium saucepan over medium heat, cook the coconut milk and chicken broth until hot. Whisk in the ginger, curry paste, and brown sugar. Add the lime leaves, turn down the heat to low, and simmer for 10 minutes.

- In a large bowl, toss the chicken with 3 tablespoons of the vegetable oil and the curry paste. Coat well. Heat a 10- or 12-inch cast iron skillet over medium-high heat. Add the remaining 1 tablespoon oil, then add the sliced ginger and cook for 1 minute. Add the chicken to the skillet, toss, and stir for 3 minutes. Add the mushrooms, bell pepper, and garlic and stir-fry for 3 to 4 minutes.

- Add the coconut sauce to the stir-fried vegetables. Add the cooked chicken and simmer for 5 minutes. Add the sugar snap peas and toss briefly to incorporate. To serve, make a bed of cooked white or brown rice on individual plates, and top each with a portion of the stir-fry and sauce. Garnish with the cashews, green onion, cilantro, and lime wedges, and serve immediately.

SAUCE

1 (14.5-ounce) can unsweetened coconut milk

1 cup chicken broth

1 teaspoon grated ginger

1 tablespoon Mae Ploy Massaman or other red curry paste

1 tablespoon brown sugar

2 kaffir lime leaves or 1 tablespoon freshly squeezed lime juice

STIR-FRY

1 pound boneless, skinless chicken breasts, cut crosswise into 1/2-by-2-inch strips

4 tablespoons vegetable oil, divided

2 tablespoons Mae Ploy Massaman or other red curry paste

5 slices fresh ginger

1 cup fresh shiitake mushrooms, stemmed and sliced

1 red bell pepper, seeded and chopped into 1/2-inch pieces

2 cloves garlic, thinly sliced

1 cup sugar snap peas, bias cut in half

GARNISH

1/2 cup roasted, salted cashews, chopped

1/4 cup chopped green onions

1/4 cup fresh cilantro leaves

6 lime wedges

mediterranean lamb shanks

This is such an easy recipe: you just have to brown the lamb shanks, add the roasted vegetable topping, and bake. The meat slowly becomes tender, and the vegetables add wonderful flavor. Serving the shanks with spaetzle and fresh asparagus is the perfect way to round out the meal.

. . . .

MAKES 4 SERVINGS

- Preheat the oven to 350°F.

- To prepare the roasted vegetable topping, combine the eggplant, peppers, garlic, and onions with the olive oil. Spoon into a 10-inch cast iron skillet and roast for 30 minutes. Remove from the oven.

- Briefly process the canned tomatoes in a food processor. Add to the roasted vegetables along with the chicken broth and vinegar. Season to taste with salt and pepper and set aside.

- To prepare the lamb, heat the olive oil in a 10-inch cast iron skillet over medium heat. Add the lamb shanks, sprinkle with rosemary, and cook for 5 to 8 minutes, turning often to brown evenly. Drain off all the fat and discard. Cover the browned lamb shanks with the roasted vegetable topping. Loosely place a piece of aluminum foil over the top; don't seal tightly or the vegetables will become mushy. Bake until the meat starts to pull away from the bone, about 2 hours. Remove the foil and bake for another 20 minutes. To serve, garnish with parsley and lemon zest. Serve with Brown Butter Spaetzle.

ROASTED VEGETABLE TOPPING

1 medium eggplant, cut into ½-inch pieces

1 red bell pepper, seeded and diced into ¼-inch pieces

½ green bell pepper, seeded and diced into ¼-inch pieces

2 cloves garlic, minced

¾ cup chopped sweet onion

3 tablespoons extra-virgin olive oil

1 (14.5-ounce) can diced tomatoes

½ cup chicken broth

¼ cup red wine vinegar

Salt and freshly ground black pepper

SEARED LAMB SHANKS

3 tablespoons olive oil

4 lamb shanks

1 tablespoon chopped fresh rosemary

2 tablespoons chopped parsley leaves, for garnish

1 teaspoon lemon zest, for garnish

. . . .

Brown Butter Spaetzle (recipe follows), for serving

brown butter spaetzle

This is a delicious accompaniment to meats, chicken, and sausages. Spaetzle can be made ahead of time, then sautéed in the brown butter just before serving. Sprinkle with a little parsley and serve.

. . . .

MAKES 4 SERVINGS

- In a large bowl, stir together the flour, eggs, milk, and 1 teaspoon salt until the mixture comes together and forms a sticky dough.

- In a large pot, bring 2 quarts water to a boil and add 1 tablespoon salt.

- Use a spaetzle maker or a potato ricer (with a ⅜-inch disk) to create the noodles. Add ½ cup batter at a time to the utensil, pressing into the boiling water. As dough comes through the hold, use a dinner knife to release the dough from the extruder. When the noodles are cooked they will rise to the surface. Use a strainer or slotted spoon to transfer the cooked spaetzle to a large bowl. If the spaetzle starts to stick together, drizzle with 1 tablespoon olive oil.

- Heat a 10- or 12-inch cast iron skillet over medium-low heat, and add 2 tablespoons of the butter. Cook until butter begins to lightly brown, about 3 minutes. Add half of the cooked spaetzle and sauté until golden, about 4 minutes. Transfer to a medium serving bowl. Add the remaining butter to the skillet, brown, and then cook the remaining spaetzle. Gently toss the noodles, sprinkle with salt, pepper, and parsley, and serve.

> 2 cups all-purpose flour
> 4 large eggs, lightly beaten
> ⅓ cup 2% or whole milk
> Salt
> 4 tablespoons unsalted butter, divided
> Freshly ground black pepper
> 2 tablespoons finely chopped parsley

jasmine tea–smoked salmon with apple-bay sauce

The original idea for tea-smoking came from Barbara Tropp, a good friend and a fantastic chef. Her recipe was for tea-smoked black cod; smoking works very well with this fish, due to its high oil content. Salmon works well too, because it is also oily, and the smoke gives it great flavor. We use jasmine tea for its floral aroma and taste, and star anise to give the dish a bit of a fennel taste. The apple-bay sauce finishes this dish nicely and balances the smokiness of the fish. Serve with a nice watercress or parsley salad.

. . . .

MAKES 4 SERVINGS

- To prepare the salmon, combine the white wine, water, sugar, salt, and ginger in a medium bowl. Add the salmon fillets, cover with plastic wrap, and refrigerate for 1 hour.

- Line the bottom of a 10- or 12-inch cast iron skillet with aluminum foil. In the center put the rice, sugar, and tea, spreading it out slightly. Put the star anise on top. Place a metal steamer basket on top of the rice mixture. Take the salmon from the marinade and pat dry. Lightly oil the steamer basket. Place the salmon fillets in a single layer in the steamer basket.

- Cut 2 large sheets of aluminum foil, each bigger than the skillet diameter, to make a generously overlapping cover for the skillet. Overlap the edges in the middle

SALMON

½ cup white wine

½ cup water

2 tablespoons sugar

2 tablespoons salt

4 thin slices ginger

1½ pounds fresh salmon fillet, skin removed, cut into 4 fillets

SMOKING THE SALMON

1 cup long-grain rice

⅔ cup sugar

⅔ cup loose jasmine or oolong tea leaves

3 star anise (optional)

. . . .

Apple-Bay Sauce (recipe follows)

2 tablespoons fresh chervil or parsley, for garnish

by about 4 inches and fold over tightly twice to seal. Then crimp down the outer edges of the foil all around the sides of the skillet so the center creates a "tent" to contain the rising smoke. Put the tightly sealed skillet over medium heat for 5 minutes. Remove the salmon from the heat and allow it to smoke off the heat for 5 minutes. Place the salmon back on the burner over medium-low heat for 5 minutes, then remove it from the heat again for 5 minutes. Repeat this process two more times for a total of 20 minutes on and off the heat. When you remove the tent the salmon should be just slightly pink in the center, and a bit of the white protein (albumin) should be showing. If the salmon is too pink for your liking, place it in the oven at 325°F for 5 minutes.

- To serve, place each portion of salmon on an individual plate with 3 to 4 tablespoons of the Apple-Bay Sauce. Sprinkle each fillet with chervil.

apple-bay sauce

MAKES ABOUT 4 CUPS

- Combine the shallot, white wine, lemon juice, and bay leaves in a nonreactive saucepan over medium heat and cook, stirring frequently, until reduced to 2 tablespoons, 3 to 5 minutes. When the reduction begins to bubble, add the cream and reduce the heat to medium-low. Add the butter, one cube at a time, whisking in on and off of the heat. Continue whisking butter into the reduction until the mixture starts to thicken. To avoid the sauce separating, do not overheat. Season with salt and pepper and stir in the apple. Remove from the heat and serve immediately.

1 shallot, finely chopped

6 to 8 ounces white wine

2 tablespoons freshly squeezed lemon juice

3 bay leaves

1 tablespoon heavy cream

¾ cup (1½ sticks) cold unsalted butter, cut into small cubes

Salt and freshly ground white pepper

1 firm, juicy apple, such as Jonagold, Gala, or Honeycrisp, peeled, cored, and finely chopped

steak and guinness pie

After a long day skiing or playing outside, we crave a warm, hearty meal. Steak and Guinness Pie is the perfect meal to warm the soul. And the best accompaniment is, of course, a glass of Guinness! If you love puff pastry as our family does, bake an extra sheet, cut into squares and place it on the bottom of the bowl, and then continue with the dish assembly.

• • • • • • • • • • • • • • • •

MAKES 6 SERVINGS

- Preheat the oven to 425°F.

- Take the puff pastry from the freezer and allow to lightly thaw (to not quite room temperature).

- Gently roll out the puff pastry to smooth any creases. Combine the egg and water in a small bowl. Place the puff pastry on a baking sheet and brush with the egg wash. Bake on the middle rack until the puff pastry is golden brown, about 25 minutes. Cut the puff pastry into 4-by-4-inch squares and set aside.

- Lower the oven temperature to 325°F.

- In a shallow dish, combine the flour, salt, and pepper. Add half of the beef cubes and dust with the flour. Shake off any excess flour. Add 1 tablespoon each of the olive oil and the butter to a 10- or 12-inch cast iron skillet over medium-high heat. Once hot, add half of the beef cubes, being sure not to crowd the pan. Cook until the meat starts to brown, about 3 minutes. Using tongs, turn the meat and cook for 3 minutes more. Transfer to a platter and repeat with

1 sheet frozen puff pastry

1 large egg, lightly beaten

1 tablespoon water

½ cup all-purpose flour

1 teaspoon salt

½ teaspoon freshly ground black pepper

1½ pounds boneless beef chuck or beef brisket, cut into 1½-inch cubes

4 tablespoons olive oil, divided

4 tablespoon unsalted butter, divided

1½ cups button mushrooms, cleaned and cut into ½-inch slices

1 medium onion, coarsely chopped

2 medium carrots, peeled and coarsely chopped

1 celery stalk, finely chopped

2 cloves garlic, chopped

2 teaspoons fresh thyme leaves

½ teaspoon dried oregano

1 cup beef broth

1 cup Guinness stout

2 tablespoons Worcestershire sauce

½ teaspoon salt

¼ teaspoon freshly ground black pepper

1½ cups grated cheddar cheese

another 1 tablespoon each of the olive oil and the butter to cook the remaining meat. Transfer to the platter.

- In the same pan, add another 1 tablespoon each of the olive oil and the butter and cook the mushrooms until they start to brown and release liquid. Transfer to a small bowl and reserve. Add the remaining olive oil and butter to the skillet, and cook the onion, carrots, and celery until the onions become translucent. Return the mushrooms to the skillet. Add the garlic, thyme, and oregano, and cook for another 2 minutes. Add the beef broth, Guinness, and Worcestershire sauce and stir. Add the beef cubes and gently mix in, coating well with the onion-mushroom mixture. Cover tightly with foil and/or a lid and place in the oven for 2 hours. Remove from the oven and season with salt and pepper.

- Serve the stew in warmed bowls, each sprinkled with cheese and topped with a puff pastry square.

seared scallops with rhubarb sauce and citrus butter glaze

We love the way scallops sear so beautifully in the cast iron skillet. The tart sweetness of the rhubarb complements the sweetness of the scallops, and the star anise is a subtle yet pleasant surprise to the palate. We love the versatility of rhubarb–it can be used for savory dishes as well as sweet. It was originally classified as a vegetable up until 1947, when the New York State Court decided to change its classification to a fruit due to its more common use in desserts and preserves.

• • • • • • • • • • • • • • • •

MAKES 6 SERVINGS

• Preheat the oven to 400°F.

• To make the sauce, put the rhubarb and 1 tablespoon of the oil in a medium bowl and toss. Spread the rhubarb over the bottom of a cast iron skillet or a baking sheet lined with parchment paper. Place on the middle rack and bake until soft enough that you can mash with the back of a spoon, about 15 minutes. Remove from the oven, set aside, and turn down the heat to 200°F.

• In a small cast iron skillet or saucepan over medium-low heat, melt 1 tablespoon of the butter. Add the leeks and sauté until soft, about 5 minutes. Put the rhubarb and leeks in a blender and blend until smooth.

2 cups rhubarb, cut into ½-inch pieces

5 tablespoons olive oil, divided, plus more as needed

4 tablespoons unsalted butter, divided

1 leek, white part only, sliced in half lengthwise, rinsed well, cut into ¼-inch slices

2 tablespoons white wine

½ cup water

3 tablespoons sugar

2 whole star anise

¼ teaspoon salt

⅛ teaspoon freshly ground white pepper

About 1¼ pounds large scallops (approximately 16)

CITRUS BUTTER

2 tablespoons unsalted butter

1 tablespoon marmalade

• Return to the saucepan and heat on medium-low. Add the wine, water, sugar, and star anise, turn the heat to low, and stir and simmer for 5 minutes. Swirl in the remaining 3 tablespoons butter, 1 tablespoon at a time. Add the salt and white pepper. Remove from the heat and reserve.

• To prepare the citrus butter, melt the butter and the marmalade in a small saucepan over medium heat. Stir well and set aside.

- To prepare the scallops, pat dry with paper towels and set on a plate. In a 10- or 12-inch cast iron skillet over medium heat, heat 2 tablespoons of the olive oil. Add the scallops without crowding, spacing them apart slightly, and cook for 2 to 3 minutes on each side. Transfer to a plate and place in the oven to keep warm. Add another 2 tablespoons olive oil and cook another batch of scallops in the same manner until all are cooked.

- Remove the scallops from the oven and brush all with the citrus butter. To serve, reheat the rhubarb sauce over low heat for 5 minutes. Place ¼ cup warm sauce on each individual plate and place 4 scallops on the sauce.

smoky smothered chicken

This delicious, golden-colored chicken offers layers of flavors, especially the smoked paprika. You can fix an easy Sunday supper and enjoy a stress-free meal. Serve with rice and a simple, light salad. The crispy onions really make this dish.

. . . .

MAKES 6 SERVINGS

- Preheat the oven to 350°F.

- Rinse the chicken and pat dry with paper towels. In a medium bowl, combine the flour, paprika, and salt. Dip the chicken in the flour mixture, lightly coating both sides. Heat 1 tablespoon each of the butter and oil in a 12-inch cast iron skillet over medium heat. Shake excess flour from the chicken, then add 5 pieces of chicken to the skillet at a time. Lightly brown the chicken for 3 minutes on each side. Transfer to a platter. Heat the remaining butter and oil and cook the remaining chicken pieces in the same manner.

- Rinse the skillet with hot water and dry with paper towels. Add the reserved chicken pieces back to the skillet. Pour the cream over the chicken. Add the garlic, jalapeño, and ginger, and gently stir to incorporate. Bake, uncovered, for 15 minutes. Turn over the chicken pieces and cook for another 15 minutes. Turn the chicken over once more, sprinkle with the onion rings, and bake for 5 minutes more. Lightly sprinkle with a few dashes of hot sauce and serve.

4 chicken thighs, boneless and skinless

3 chicken breasts, boneless and skinless, cut in half crosswise

½ cup all-purpose flour

1 tablespoon smoked paprika

1 teaspoon salt

2 tablespoons unsalted butter, divided

2 tablespoons olive oil, divided

1 cup heavy cream

2 cloves garlic, minced

1 tablespoon finely diced jalapeño pepper, seeds removed

¼ cup finely chopped candied ginger

⅔ cup French's or other brand fried onion rings

Hot sauce, preferably Crystal (optional)

seared rib-eye with truffle butter and rogue river smoked blue cheese

The rib-eye steak has so much flavor. Searing it in the cast iron skillet forms a crisp crust and seals in the juices. Searing also cooks out the excess fat. At our house, it's the favorite steak.

. . . .

MAKES 4 SERVINGS

- To prepare the truffle butter, combine the shallots, butter, truffle salt, and parsley in a small bowl.

- Preheat the oven to 375°F.

- Heat a 12-inch cast iron skillet over medium-high heat. Add the olive oil. Season both sides of the steaks with salt and pepper. Cook the steaks for 3 minutes on each side, then transfer to the oven and bake for 5 minutes to finish cooking. Remove from the pan, let the steaks rest for 5 minutes, spread with truffle butter, and cut into ¾-inch-thick slices. Sprinkle the crumbled blue cheese over the sliced steak. Serve with Butter-Mashed Yukon Gold Potatoes.

1 tablespoon minced shallot

4 tablespoons unsalted butter, at room temperature

1 teaspoon truffle salt

1 tablespoon minced parsley

1 tablespoon olive oil

2 rib-eye steaks

Salt and freshly ground black pepper

2 ounces Rogue River smoked blue cheese, crumbled

Butter-Mashed Yukon Gold Potatoes (recipe follows)

butter-mashed yukon gold potatoes

MAKES 4 TO 6 SERVINGS

* In a large pot, cover the potatoes with cold salted water. Bring to a boil and cook for 20 minutes. Drain the potatoes. Warm a 10- or 12-inch cast iron skillet over medium heat. Put the potatoes in the skillet and partially mash with a

2 pounds Yukon Gold potatoes, peeled and quartered

¼ cup unsalted butter

½ cup sour cream

Salt and freshly ground black pepper

potato masher. Add the butter, sour cream, salt, and pepper. Cook over medium heat, stirring with a wooden spoon, until the butter is melted and the potatoes are creamy and still slightly chunky. Serve hot.

peppers and roasted sausages with sweet and sour sauerkraut slaw

A cast iron skillet of sausages and another skillet of roasted onions and peppers served with several mustards and French rolls can make an easy meal for a gathering of friends.

. . . .

MAKES 6 SERVINGS

- Preheat the oven to 375°F.

- Swirl 2 tablespoons of the olive oil in a 10-inch cast iron skillet. Arrange the sausage in the skillet and place in the oven.

- In a second cast iron skillet, arrange the pepper strips and onions and drizzle with the remaining 3 tablespoons olive oil.

5 tablespoons extra-virgin olive oil, divided
2 pounds Italian sausage
3 red bell peppers, seeded, each cut into 8 strips
1 sweet yellow onion, cut in half and sliced
6 crusty French rolls
Sweet and Sour Sauerkraut Slaw (recipe follows)

Place in the oven. Roast the sausages and pepper-onion mixture for 20 minutes, then turn over and cook for another 15 minutes. Serve with the crusty French rolls for guests to fill themselves and with a few spoonfuls of Sweet and Sour Sauerkraut Slaw.

sweet and sour sauerkraut slaw

Make this slaw at least a few hours ahead, preferably overnight. Store in the refrigerator.

· · · · · · · · · · · · · · · · · ·

MAKES 6 CUPS

• Combine the sauerkraut, celery, bell peppers, and green onions in a large bowl and mix well. Whisk together the sugar, oil, and vinegar, and pour over the vegetables. Stir well and refrigerate.

4 cups sauerkraut, well drained
1 cup chopped celery
½ cup chopped red bell pepper
½ cup chopped green bell pepper
1 cup chopped green onions
1 cup sugar
¼ cup vegetable oil
¾ cup white vinegar

SMOKED SALMON HASH WITH
TRICOLORED POTATOES, PAGE 5

APPLE FRENCH TOAST BREAD PUDDING, PAGE 12

ROASTED POBLANO AND
CRAB HUSH PUPPIES, PAGE 34

SIZZLING SHRIMP, PAGE 41

SKILLET-ROASTED MUSSELS, PAGE 60

CHICKEN AND CASHEW RED CURRY, PAGE 65

STEAK AND GUINNESS PIE, PAGE 70

SEARED RIB-EYE WITH TRUFFLE BUTTER AND
ROGUE RIVER SMOKED BLUE CHEESE, PAGE 75

TAMARIND-GLAZED CRAB, PAGE 82

LAMB CHOPS WITH CHIMICHURRI SAUCE, PAGE 89

CARAMELIZED FENNEL, SHALLOT, AND PEAR UPSIDE-DOWN TART, PAGE 95

GOLDEN CURRY CAULIFLOWER, PAGE 102

PEACH BLUEBERRY CORNMEAL COBBLER, PAGE 135

SPICY APPLE CAKE, PAGE 138

lemon chicken sofrito

Sofrito, which means "lightly fried," is a favorite cooking base for many dishes in Spanish cuisine; it's a sautéed vegetable mixture used as a sauce. For another variation you can add diced tomatoes. We have added garam masala because we like the flavor it adds to this dish. The chicken gets golden brown (but stays moist and tender) in the skillet, and the lemon juice and olives blend together to add zest to the dish.

. . . .

MAKES 4 SERVINGS

- Preheat the oven to 375°F.

- To prepare the sofrito, in a 10- or 12-inch cast iron skillet over medium heat, warm 3 tablespoons of the olive oil. Add the onions, garlic, and bell pepper and sauté briefly. Add the lemon juice and wine and simmer for 3 minutes. Transfer to a small bowl.

- In a medium bowl, toss the olives and artichokes with 2 tablespoons of the olive oil.

- Clean the skillet, then warm it over medium heat and add the remaining 3 tablespoons olive oil. Brown the chicken on both sides. Sprinkle with the garam masala, salt, and pepper. Spoon the sofrito over the chicken, then scatter the olives and artichoke hearts into the skillet and bake, uncovered, for 25 minutes. Add the lemon wedges, and bake for 15 minutes more. Sprinkle with chopped parsley and serve.

½ cup extra-virgin olive oil, divided

¾ cup chopped yellow onion

1 tablespoon minced garlic

¾ cup diced red bell pepper

Freshly squeezed juice of 1 lemon

½ cup dry white wine

3 chicken breasts, skin on, bone in, cut in half crosswise

1 teaspoon Garam Masala (see page 56)

Salt and freshly ground black pepper

8 to 10 pimiento-stuffed jumbo green olives

1 (8-ounce) package frozen (thawed) artichoke hearts

1 lemon, cut in half lengthwise, sliced into six ½-inch wedges

1 tablespoon chopped fresh parsley leaves, for garnish

salty, sweet, and spicy flank steak

We love flank steak on the barbecue, but on rainy days when cooking outdoors just doesn't sound inviting, we cut up a flank steak and take advantage of the cast iron skillet. The meat gets nice and crispy all over, with a juicy, flavorful interior. It's also delicious the next day, cold on a salad or wrapped up in a tortilla with your favorite salsa, thinly sliced iceberg lettuce, cilantro, and avocado. Our families love a creamy avocado-cilantro sauce drizzled over the top.

MAKES 6 SERVINGS

- Prepare the marinade: In a medium bowl, combine the honey and hot water to form a thin liquid. Add the soy sauce, garlic, vinegar, garam masala, minced ginger, pepper flakes, cornstarch, and canola and sesame oils, and mix well.

- Put the steak in a nonreactive bowl or large zip-locking bag with the marinade and refrigerate for 2 to 3 hours.

- When ready to cook the steak, place a strainer in the sink and drain off the marinade. Put the steak in a bowl. In a cast iron skillet over medium-heat, add 2 tablespoons of the olive oil and the ginger slices and heat until the ginger gives off fragrance and the oil starts to sputter. Add the steak, making sure not to crowd the pan, and cook for 2 minutes. Stir or flip the steaks with tongs and cook for another 2 to 3 minutes. Transfer to a plate and repeat with the rest of the steak, using 2 more tablespoons of oil for each batch. Add the carrots to the skillet and toss, then return the cooked steak to the skillet and cook for another 2 to 3 minutes. Remove from the heat and add the scallions. Serve hot with rice and Creamy Avocado-Cilantro Sauce.

2 tablespoons honey

2 tablespoons hot water

¼ cup soy sauce

2 cloves garlic, minced

3 tablespoons black rice wine vinegar or Worcestershire sauce

1 tablespoon Garam Masala (see page 56)

2 teaspoons fresh ginger, peeled and minced, or 1 teaspoon ginger paste

¼ teaspoon crushed hot pepper flakes

1 tablespoon cornstarch

1 tablespoons canola or other vegetable oil

1 teaspoon light or dark sesame oil (optional)

1½ pounds flank steak, cut across the grain into ½-by-3-inch slices

6 tablespoons olive oil or other vegetable oil, divided

3 slices fresh ginger

2 medium carrots, peeled, cut in half lengthwise, then in matchsticks with a mandoline, or coarsely grated

1 bunch scallions, white and green parts, cut lengthwise into 3-inch-long strips

6 cups steamed white or brown rice

Creamy Avocado-Cilantro Sauce (recipe follows)

creamy avocado-cilantro sauce

MAKES 2 CUPS

• Combine all the ingredients in a blender and blend until well combined. Pour into a bowl and serve drizzled over the flank steak.

1 avocado

2 cloves garlic

¼ cup packed cilantro leaves

2 tablespoons lime juice

⅔ cup plain yogurt

2 tablespoons mayonnaise

2 tablespoons water

1 teaspoon hot sauce, preferably Crystal or Tabasco

Salt and freshly ground black pepper

tamarind-glazed crab

This crab is a bit messy, but so delicious. The flavors hit all the senses: spicy, sweet, hot, and salty.

. . . .

MAKES A GREAT APPETIZER FOR 4 PEOPLE

- To prepare the sauce, place all the ingredients in a small sauté pan and bring to a boil, stirring until the sugar is dissolved and well combined. Turn off the heat and set aside.

- To prepare the crab, remove the triangular-shaped belly flap or apron. Turn over and remove the outer shell by inserting your thumb between the body and shell at the rear of the crab and pulling the shell up. Remove the gills and roe or "crab butter." Remove the spongy gills and small paddles (beak) and discard. Break each crab into two pieces: holding the crab body facing up and away from you, force both halves upward, breaking the crab body in half. Pull the crab legs from the body and break each half-body in half again, quartering the body meat. Let the pieces dry completely on a plate lined with paper towels.

TAMARIND-GINGER SAUCE

4 ounces tamarind paste

1 cup water

⅔ cup hoisin sauce

½ cup oyster sauce

¾ cup sugar

5 slices ginger

GLAZED CRAB

2 whole Dungeness crabs, 2 to 3 pounds each, cooked

¼ cup vegetable oil

1 or 2 Thai bird chilies, sliced down one side and smashed lightly with the flat edge of a knife, retaining the seeds

4 scallions, green and white parts, cut into 3-inch-long strips

2 cloves garlic, minced

½ teaspoon salt

Lemon wedges, for serving

Asian Slaw (recipe follows), for serving

- In a 10- or 12-inch cast iron skillet over medium-high heat, heat the vegetable oil. When hot, add the crab and cook for 3 minutes. With tongs, turn the crab and cook for 3 minutes more. Add the chilies and half the scallions. Add 1½ cups of the tamarind sauce and the garlic, turning several times to coat the crab completely. Serve directly from the skillet or place on a platter and sprinkle the remaining scallions and salt. Provide guests with bowls of warm water, each with a lemon wedge, and plenty of napkins. Serve with extra sauce on the side, steamed rice, and Asian Slaw.

asian slaw

MAKES 6 SERVINGS

- To make the dressing, in a small bowl, whisk together all the ingredients except for the Thai chile. Gently stir in the chile. Allow the mixture to sit for 15 minutes.

- To make the slaw, in a large bowl, combine all the ingredients and toss well.

- Remove the chilies from the dressing and discard (if you prefer more heat, transfer a few slices to a cutting board and finely dice before returning to the dressing). Pour the dressing over the slaw and toss well to coat.

NUOC CHAM DRESSING

3 tablespoons lime juice

2 tablespoons sugar

2 tablespoons orange juice

3 tablespoons rice wine vinegar

2½ tablespoons fish sauce

¼ teaspoon sesame oil

1 tablespoon safflower or vegetable oil

½ Thai chile, sliced

SLAW

5 cups Napa cabbage, cut into ½-inch pieces

1 carrot, shredded or julienned

½ red pepper, seeded, cut into thin strips and cut in half

¼ cup chopped, roasted peanuts

3 tablespoons Thai basil leaves, thinly sliced

2 tablespoons fresh cilantro leaves

tinga poblana with beef

We like to use this spicy and flavorful beef as a filling for tacos. Serve in warm tortillas topped with finely shredded cabbage, sour cream, and avocado, and dressed with freshly squeezed lime juice. A chicken variation is also tasty: substitute cooked rotisserie chicken meat for the cooked beef and add 1 cup chicken broth.

. . . .

MAKES 6 SERVINGS

- Preheat the oven to 325°F.

- In a 10- or 12-inch cast iron skillet, heat the oil over medium-high heat and brown the beef. Add the water, cover, and bake until tender, 1½ to 2 hours. Transfer the meat from the skillet. Reserve the broth. Using 2 forks, shred the meat and set aside.

- In the same skillet, cook the chorizo, onion, and garlic. Add the shredded beef, tomatoes, chilies, oregano, and sugar. Add ¾ cup of the reserved broth and simmer for 30 minutes. Season to taste with salt and pepper. Serve with tortillas, cabbage, avocado, sour cream, and limes.

2 tablespoons vegetable oil

1½ pounds boneless beef chuck, trimmed and cut into 2-inch pieces

1 cup water

½ pound uncooked Mexican chorizo, casing removed

1 cup chopped white onion

3 cloves garlic, chopped

1 (14.5-ounce) can diced tomatoes, drained

2 canned chipotle chilies in adobo sauce

1 teaspoon dried oregano

1 teaspoon sugar

Salt and freshly ground black pepper

12 (8-inch) flour or corn tortillas, for serving

4 cups shredded cabbage, for serving

1 avocado, diced, for serving

½ cup sour cream, for serving

2 limes, quartered, for serving

yakisoba with shrimp and fresh vegetables

Yakisoba means "fried noodles." The skillet's wide surface area allows the noodles to fry without stewing. Buying precooked noodles saves a step, and we add the vegetables right at the end so they stay fresh and crisp. The sauce flavors the noodles and is a good balance of sweet and hot, with just a little salt.

. . . .

MAKES 2 SERVINGS

- To prepare the sauce, in a small bowl, combine all the ingredients until well blended and set aside.

- To prepare the noodles, heat a 10-inch cast iron skillet over medium heat. Add the vegetable oil, then add the noodles, breaking apart with 2 forks. Add the water, cover, and cook for 3 minutes. Uncover the skillet and stir in the bell pepper, carrots, cabbage, and prawns. Spoon 4 to 5 tablespoons of the sauce over the top and quickly mix in. Garnish with the green onions and sesame seeds and drizzle the remaining sauce over the top. Serve with soy sauce.

SAUCE

1 teaspoon brown sugar

2 tablespoons soy sauce

2 tablespoons hoisin sauce

1 tablespoon ketchup

1 teaspoon sriracha sauce (optional)

3 tablespoons Worcestershire sauce

YAKISOBA

2 tablespoons vegetable oil

½ pound fully cooked yakisoba noodles (available at large grocery stores and Asian markets)

¼ cup water

½ red bell pepper, cut into ½-by-¼-inch strips

1 cup shredded carrots, blanched

1 cup finely shredded green cabbage

½ pound fully cooked, peeled prawns (26 to 30 per pound), cut into thirds, tails removed

¼ cup chopped green onions, for garnish

Toasted sesame seeds, for garnish

Soy sauce, for serving

seared salmon with roasted tomato, olive, and bacon relish

Summertime gives us an abundance of sweet little cherry tomatoes. These, plus celery and onion, simply roasted in the cast iron skillet, are the base for this flavorful relish, which also goes great with chicken. For a delightful contrast of textures, we suggest the accompaniment of an orange, shaved fennel, and beet salad. The baking time of the salmon will depend on the thickness of your fillet—the general rule is to cook for 8 to 10 minutes per inch of thickness.

. . . .

MAKES 4 SERVINGS

- Preheat the oven to 400°F.

- To prepare the relish, place the bacon on a foil-lined baking sheet and bake until crisp, 10 to 12 minutes. Transfer to paper towels and, when cool, coarsely chop.

- Add the cherry tomatoes and the celery and onion to a 10- or 12-inch cast iron skillet. Drizzle with the olive oil and sprinkle with the salt and pepper. Toss gently and roast in the oven for 20 minutes. Remove from the oven and cool slightly. Transfer to a medium bowl. Add the cooked bacon and the olives, vinegar, and brown sugar and toss to coat. Set the relish aside.

- To prepare the salmon, in a small bowl, combine the salt, brown sugar, lemon zest, and garam masala. Lightly rub the salmon fillets with 1 tablespoon of the olive oil and sprinkle the fillets with the pepper and the seasoning mixture.

RELISH

8 strips bacon

2 cups cherry tomatoes

4 stalks celery, chopped

½ yellow onion, chopped

3 tablespoons olive oil

1½ teaspoons kosher salt

¼ teaspoon freshly ground black pepper

½ cup pitted, chopped kalamata olives

2 tablespoons balsamic vinegar

1 tablespoon brown sugar

. . . .

1 teaspoon kosher salt

1 tablespoon brown sugar

Zest of 1 lemon

1 teaspoon Garam Masala (see page 56)

4 salmon fillets, skin on

2 tablespoons olive oil, divided

¼ teaspoon freshly ground black pepper

- Heat the remaining 1 tablespoon olive oil in a 10- or 12-inch cast iron skillet over medium-high heat. Add the salmon fillets, skin side down, and cook for 3 to 4 minutes. Transfer to the oven and cook for another 10 minutes. Remove from the oven, top each serving with 2 to 3 tablespoons relish, and serve.

lynn's no-bean chili

Our dear friend Lynn Nelson made this no-bean chili for us on Halloween, and it was so delicious. The meat melts in your mouth and is a nice change from the traditional chili. Serve with corn bread. Our family also likes to add this to a baked potato!

. . . .

MAKES 6 SERVINGS

- In a 10- to 12-inch cast iron skillet over medium heat, cook the bacon, stirring until crisp. Add the onions and garlic and cook, stirring, until the onions are softened. Add the chili powder, smoked paprika, and cumin and cook, stirring, for 2 minutes. Add the beef, water, and oregano, and simmer, uncovered, adding more water if necessary to keep the beef barely covered, until the beef is tender, 2 to 2½ hours. Add the salt and pepper and stir. Stir in the cornmeal and simmer the chili, stirring occasionally, for 5 minutes, or until it is thickened slightly. Serve in bowls with sour cream on the table.

3 slices bacon, chopped

1 large onion, chopped

3 cloves garlic, minced

3 tablespoons chili powder

½ teaspoon smoked paprika

2 teaspoons ground cumin

2½ pounds rib-eye steak, cut into ½-inch pieces

3½ cups water

1 teaspoon dried oregano, crumbled

1 teaspoon salt

¼ teaspoon freshly ground black pepper

1 tablespoon cornmeal

¼ cup sour cream, for garnish

spaghetti carbonara

This pasta dish is such a favorite, in part because you can keep the ingredients on hand and quickly fix a light dinner or late-night snack. Tossing the cooked pasta with the bacon, oil, and butter mixture before adding the eggs and cheese will help prevent the egg from scrambling. The bacon adds a great flavor to the dish. We include fresh peas and a little cream—it's not traditional, but we prefer it. We also frequently use penne rigate in the place of spaghetti.

. . . .

MAKES 4 SERVINGS

- Fill a large pot with 4 quarts of water and bring to a boil. When the water boils, add the peas and cook for 1 minute. Remove with a strainer or slotted spoon and transfer to a small bowl. Stir in the salt. Bring the water back to a boil, then add the spaghetti. Cook just until al dente. Reserve ⅔ cup of the cooking water, then drain the spaghetti.

- Meanwhile, warm a 12-inch cast iron skillet over medium-low heat and cook the chopped bacon just until it begins to crisp and turn golden brown. Pour off all but 2 tablespoons of the fat.

½ cup freshly shelled peas

1 tablespoon salt

12 ounces spaghetti

5 slices of thick-sliced bacon, cut crosswise into ½-inch strips

3 tablespoons unsalted butter, softened

3 tablespoons olive oil

2 large eggs, beaten

⅓ cup heavy cream

1 cup freshly grated Parmesan cheese

Freshly ground black pepper

- Add the butter and olive oil to the skillet along with the hot cooked spaghetti. Coat the noodles with the bacon and oil. Work quickly so the pasta stays hot. Add a little of the pasta cooking water to the noodles to keep them from becoming too dry. Stir in the eggs and cream. Remove from the heat and mix well. Sprinkle with the cheese and peas. Serve immediately with lots of pepper.

lamb chops with chimichurri sauce

This bright green Argentinian sauce with red pepper is a popular condiment to serve with meats and seafood. Serve the lamb chops hot from the skillet with the chimichurri sauce drizzled over the meat. You can also use a rack of lamb cut into individual chops and seared in the same manner.

• • • • • • • • • • • • • • • • • •

MAKES 4 SERVINGS

- To prepare the sauce, in a small bowl combine the bell pepper, oil, vinegar, lemon juice, shallots, pepper flakes, salt, and honey. Let sit for 1 hour at room temperature to let the flavors mingle. Just before serving, add the parsley and mint.

- Preheat the oven to 350°F.

- Heat a 12-inch cast iron skillet over medium-high heat. Add the oil and swirl around the pan to evenly coat. Sprinkle the lamb chops with salt and pepper. When the pan is hot, add the chops. Sear for 5 minutes on each side. Transfer to the oven and finish cooking for 10 minutes. If you are using individual rib chops, sear for 3 minutes on each side, place in the oven for 5 minutes to finish cooking, and serve right from the skillet.

½ cup red bell pepper, seeded and finely chopped
½ cup extra-virgin olive oil
¼ cup red wine vinegar
2 tablespoons freshly squeezed lemon juice
2 tablespoons minced shallot
¼ teaspoon dried red pepper flakes
½ teaspoon sea salt
1 teaspoon honey
½ cup finely chopped fresh parsley
2 tablespoons fresh mint, finely chopped
2 to 3 tablespoons extra-virgin olive oil
8 (1-inch-thick) lamb loin chops
Salt and freshly ground black pepper

on the side

SIDE DISHES CAN MAKE THE MEAL WHEN PAIRED WITH THE RIGHT COMPLEMENTARY main dish. We rely on our taste memory to help us when we are planning our menu. *Keep it simple* is our mantra. James Beard said that "a menu should consist of a cold first course, an entrée with a side dish, and a seasonal dessert." Our first thought is always "What's in season?" Fresh asparagus and hot-pink rhubarb shout out SPRING! A platter of roasted fresh asparagus can hold its own next to any main dish. And in August, ripe tomatoes and just-picked sweet corn fill our baskets. We never plan a menu too far ahead because it all depends on what looks good at the market that day. If you're in the mood for a simple roasted chicken, the Caramelized Fennel, Shallot, and Pear Upside-Down Tart can dress up the plate, and the flavors complement the chicken beautifully. Try Dad's Hot Slaw with Bacon and the Crispy Red Potatoes with grilled salmon. The Skillet-Baked Polenta with White Cheddar will soak up all the delicious juices from braised short ribs, and Roasted Brussels Sprouts and Yukon Gold Potatoes with Crispy Pancetta complete the menu. And lamb chops are wonderful when accompanied by Golden Curry Cauliflower. Side dishes should be interesting enough to share center stage with the main dish. Cooked and sometimes presented in the cast iron skillet, they tempt you to dish up!

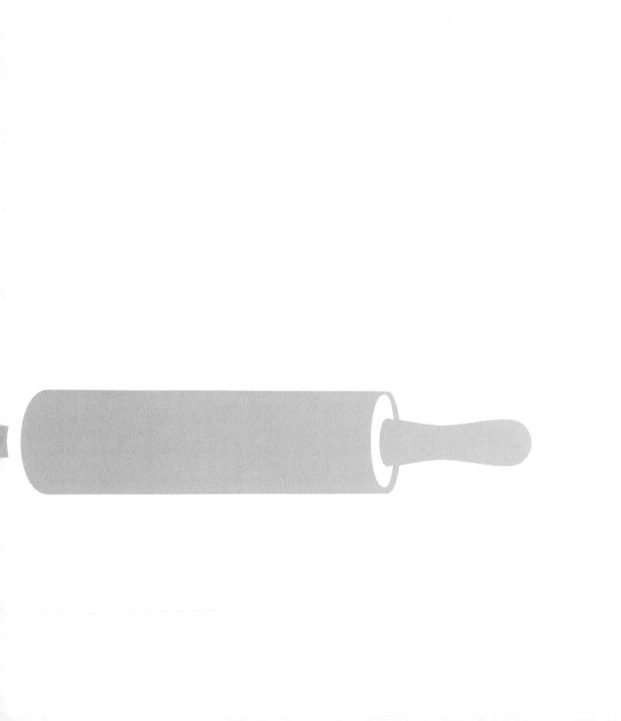

caramelized fennel, shallot, and pear upside-down tart

This is a nice combination of savory and sweet. It makes a wonderful appetizer or a side dish. Try it with white cheddar cheese instead of blue cheese, too.

. . . .

MAKES 6 TO 8 SERVINGS

1 sheet puff pastry, frozen

3 large shallots, peeled, root ends trimmed (keeping the base intact), and cut lengthwise into thirds

4 tablespoons unsalted butter, divided

1½ fennel bulbs, white bulb only, cut in half lengthwise, root trimmed, sliced into 1-inch pieces

1 cup apple cider

3 tablespoons Pernod (anise-flavored liqueur)

3 tablespoons sugar

1 red or yellow Bartlett pear, cored and cut lengthwise into 2-inch slices

1 teaspoon fresh thyme leaves

½ cup crumbled blue cheese

½ teaspoon salt

¼ teaspoon freshly ground black pepper

- Preheat the oven to 425°F. Pull the puff pastry from the freezer.

- In a small saucepan, bring 2 cups water to a boil, add the shallots, and turn down the heat to medium or a gentle boil. Cook for 8 to 10 minutes. Drain, place on a paper towel, and set aside.

- In a 10- or 12-inch cast iron skillet, melt 2 tablespoons of the butter over medium heat. Add the fennel and cook for 3 to 4 minutes. Add the apple cider, Pernod, and sugar and cover with a lid for 8 minutes. Uncover and cook on medium-high heat until the cider is reduced and the fennel has softened, about 5 minutes. Cut fennel slices in half, keeping layered sections intact. Place fennel sections around the pan, leaving spaces for the shallots and pear. Add 1 tablespoon of the butter and allow it to melt. Add the pear slices, tucking them between the fennel bulbs. Fill in any open spaces with shallots. Cut the remaining 1 tablespoon butter in half and place on top of the fruit and vegetables. Heat over medium heat until the pears and shallots start to caramelize, about 5 minutes. Remove from the heat and let cool slightly. Sprinkle with the fresh thyme and ¼ cup of the blue cheese. Season with salt and pepper.

- On a lightly floured surface, gently roll out the puff pastry. Trim the corners slightly. It will shrink up a bit when baked. Carefully place the puff pastry on top of the fennel mixture. Cook for 10 minutes. Reduce the oven temperature to 400°F and cook until golden brown, about 15 minutes more. Serve warm or at room temperature.

sweet potato gratin with garam masala

Today sweet potatoes are becoming more popular and are no longer reserved for the holidays. This is a perfect accompaniment for barbecue ribs, grilled chicken, or pork tenderloin. The gratin turns out with beautiful layers of sweet potatoes and custard filling in between. It tastes a bit like pumpkin pie.

. . . .

MAKES 6 TO 8 SERVINGS

- Preheat oven to 375°F. Butter a 10-inch cast iron skillet.

- In a medium bowl, whisk together the cream, garam masala, ginger, egg yolks, and salt. Arrange one-third of the sweet potato slices in 1 layer in the skillet. Pour 1 cup of the cream mixture over the top. Layer another third of the sweet potatoes, then pour ½ cup of the cream mixture over the top. Add the final third of the sweet potatoes, pour the remaining cream mixture over the top. Dot with the butter and season with salt and pepper. Cover with foil and bake for 20 minutes.

- Increase the oven temperature to 425°F. Uncover the gratin and bake for another 15 minutes, or until the potatoes are soft and easily pierced with a fork.

1 tablespoon unsalted butter, softened

1½ cups heavy cream

1 teaspoons Garam Masala (see page 56)

3 egg yolks

½ teaspoon kosher salt

2 large sweet potatoes, peeled and sliced ⅛ inch thick

1 tablespoon cold unsalted butter, cut into small pieces

Freshly ground black pepper

roasted broccoli with golden peppers, pine nuts, and raisins

This is a colorful vegetable dish with lots of flavor, especially from the roasted peppers. It's a good accompaniment for a seared salmon dinner.

. . . .

MAKES 4 SERVINGS

- Preheat the oven to 375°F.

- In a 10-inch cast iron skillet, coat the broccoli, pepper strips, and garlic slices with the olive oil. Add the pine nuts, raisins, red pepper flakes, and lemon zest. Season with salt and pepper and bake for 25 minutes. Serve warm.

1 pound broccoli, trimmed and broken into small pieces

1 yellow bell pepper, seeded and cut into 8 strips, each 2 inches wide

1 orange bell pepper seeded and cut into 8 strips, each 2 inches wide

2 cloves garlic, sliced

¼ cup olive oil

¼ cup pine nuts

½ cup golden raisins, soaked briefly in hot water and drained

Pinch of red pepper flakes

2 teaspoons lemon zest

Salt and freshly ground black pepper

dad's hot slaw with bacon

This is a family favorite created by Sharon's dad/Julie's grandpa. He won his Great Chefs of the West cook's hat with this recipe. The anchovies dissolve in the hot dressing, which is then stirred into the shredded cabbage, for a tangy blend of salty, savory, and crunchy-sweet cabbage. This side dish is excellent with steaks or seared fish.

. . . .

MAKES 4 SERVINGS

- Cut the bacon into 2-inch pieces and cook in a 10- to 12-inch cast iron skillet over medium heat. Transfer the bacon to a paper towel and reserve. Wipe out the skillet. Heat the olive oil in the skillet over medium heat. Add the vinegar, anchovies, and garlic. Mash the anchovies with a fork until dissolved. Turn up the heat and cook just until the mixture begins to boil. Stir in the shredded cabbage and cook for 1 to 2 minutes. Transfer to a serving bowl. Sprinkle with the bacon, season well with pepper, and serve immediately.

6 slices bacon
⅓ cup olive oil
⅓ cup red wine vinegar
1 small tin flat anchovies
2 cloves garlic, thinly sliced
½ head green cabbage, shredded
Freshly ground black pepper

potato gratin with crisp prosciutto strips

The ninety-minute baking time yields a soft, creamy potato gratin. The prosciutto strips add extra flavor.

. . . .

MAKES 6 SERVINGS

- Preheat the oven to 350°F.

- Butter a 10-inch cast iron skillet with 1 tablespoon of the butter. Arrange one-third of the potatoes evenly in the pan. Season with salt and pepper. Add half of the cheese. Repeat with another third of the potatoes, adding the remaining cheese. Finish with the final third of the potatoes. Pour the half-and-half over the mixture. Season with salt and pepper and dot the top with the remaining butter. Bake for 45 minutes.

2 tablespoons salted butter

3 large russet potatoes, peeled and sliced very thin, like potato chips

Salt and freshly ground black pepper

½ pound Taleggio cheese, rind removed and cut into ½-inch slices, or 2 cups grated Gruyère

1½ cups half-and-half

½ cup heavy cream

3 ounces thin-sliced prosciutto, cut crosswise into ½-inch strips

- Remove from the oven and pour the heavy cream evenly over the top of the cooked potatoes. Return to the oven and bake 30 minutes more. Sprinkle the prosciutto strips over the top and finish baking for 10 more minutes.

razor clam kedgeree

Kedgeree is believed to have come from Scotland to India—or so some say. This is James Beard's version that he taught at his summer cooking classes at Seaside, Oregon, which we were fortunate enough to attend. You can substitute chopped clams or smoked salmon. Razor clams also make an incredible chowder. We buy ours from the local farmers market in Olympia, Washington.

Note: For instructions on cleaning razor clams, visit www.westportwa.com/activities/razorclams/cleaning.html. Westport, Washington, is one of many cities on the West Coast known for its clam digs.

MAKES 4 SERVINGS

- Sauté the onion in 4 tablespoons of the butter in a 10- or 12-inch cast iron skillet over moderate heat. Stir in the curry powder and cook for several minutes. Add the rice and mix well with the chopped onions and curry. Melt the remaining butter and pour it over the chopped razor clams. Mix well. Stir in the curried rice. Cook just long enough to heat through. Sprinkle with the parsley, hard-boiled eggs, and green onions and serve.

½ cup chopped onion

6 tablespoons unsalted butter, divided

1 teaspoon curry powder

3 cups cooked long-grain rice

1 cup cleaned and chopped razor clams

2 tablespoons minced parsley

2 hard-boiled eggs, chopped

¼ cup sliced green onions

frizzled kale and golden beets

This is an amazing crispy treat and tastes great with roasted chicken. It also makes a nice healthy snack that even the kids love! The sweet beets taste like candy and add a pop of color. The beets can be roasted a day ahead and reheated before serving with the kale.

. . . .

MAKES 4 SERVINGS

- Preheat the oven to 425°F.

- Toss the beets with the oil and sprinkle with salt and pepper. Wrap with aluminum foil and bake in the oven for 35 to 40 minutes, or until tender.

- After beets have been in the oven for 25 minutes, cut the larger leaves of kale into 2-inch pieces. Lightly toss with the olive oil and sprinkle with the salt, pepper, and nutmeg. Place in a cast iron skillet in the oven for 15 minutes or until the kale is airy and crispy.

- Allow the beets to cool slightly, then peel them, trimming as needed, and cut into ½-inch wedges. Place in a large bowl. Drizzle with the olive oil and balsamic vinegar, and toss. Sprinkle with the salt, pepper, dill, and goat cheese. Serve with the frizzled kale.

ROASTED BEETS

3 to 4 golden beets, greens removed and roots trimmed

1 tablespoon olive oil

Salt and freshly ground black pepper

FRIZZLED KALE

1 bunch purple kale, leaves folded in half and thick stem and rib removed

1 tablespoon olive oil

½ teaspoon salt

¼ teaspoon freshly ground black pepper

⅛ teaspoon freshly grated nutmeg

DRESSING

2 tablespoons olive oil

2 tablespoons balsamic vinegar

¼ teaspoon salt

¼ teaspoon freshly ground black pepper

2 teaspoons fresh chopped dill

3 tablespoons fresh goat cheese, crumbled

golden curry cauliflower

Tony Ring, a regional chef for the Pacific Northwest group of Anthony's Restaurants, created this delicious way to cook cauliflower. Even those who don't usually favor cauliflower like this preparation.

• • • • • • • • • • • • • • • •

MAKES 4 SERVINGS

- Preheat the oven to 400°F.

- In a large bowl, roll the cauliflower in the melted butter until evenly coated. Blend the sugar, curry powder, turmeric, paprika, and salt; sprinkle over the butter-coated cauliflower. Stir to evenly coat. Spread out evenly in a 10-inch cast iron skillet. Bake for 10 minutes, then turn the cauliflower pieces with a spatula. Return to the oven and cook until the cauliflower is tender and golden, 10 minutes more. Transfer to a serving dish and serve warm.

1 head cauliflower, florets removed from the core, larger florets cut in half

4 tablespoons unsalted butter, melted

1 tablespoon sugar

1 tablespoon curry powder

½ teaspoon turmeric

½ teaspoon smoked paprika

1 teaspoon kosher salt

brown butter sage balls

Potatoes the size of large marbles are boiled and then browned in butter with fresh sage. They make a good appetizer or side dish. We like them with the Lemon Chicken Sofrito (page 79) and Frizzled Kale and Golden Beets (page 101).

MAKES 6 SERVINGS

- Preheat the oven to 375°F.

- Boil the potatoes in a pot of well-salted water until fork tender, about 12 minutes. Drain. Heat a 10- or 12-inch cast iron skillet over medium heat. Add the butter and cook for 1 minute. As the foam subsides, add the sage and stir. Add the potatoes and the salt and pepper and stir. Let cook, untouched, for 3 to 5 minutes. Transfer the skillet to the oven and cook for 10 minutes more. Taste and add salt and pepper if needed.

2 pounds small round potatoes
4 tablespoons unsalted butter, cut into 4 pieces
2 tablespoons chopped fresh sage
1 teaspoon sea salt or kosher salt
Freshly ground black pepper

roasted asparagus with citrus and parmesan

This is an easy and tasty recipe for asparagus. We love how the asparagus tips get crispy. Serve this dish with lamb or salmon.

• • • • • • • • • • • • • • • •

MAKES 4 SERVINGS

- Preheat the oven to 425°F.

- Put the asparagus in a 10- to 12-inch cast iron skillet and drizzle with the olive oil. Sprinkle with the salt, pepper, lemon zest, and Parmesan. Toss to coat and place in the hot oven.

- Bake for 8 to 10 minutes. Remove from the oven, sprinkle with the fleur de sel, and serve.

1 pound asparagus, ends trimmed

2 tablespoons extra-virgin olive oil

1 teaspoon salt

¼ teaspoon freshly ground black pepper

1 teaspoon freshly grated lemon zest

3 tablespoons freshly grated Parmesan cheese

½ teaspoon fleur de sel or kosher salt

braised carrots with citrus butter

Braising the carrots slowly brings out their sweetness and creates a beautiful, shiny glaze. The caraway and ginger add a unique and complementary flavor.

. . . .

MAKES 6 SERVINGS

- Place the carrots in a 10- or 12-inch cast iron skillet. Add 1 cup water and the butter, zest, and juice. Simmer over medium-low heat for 20 minutes, stirring several times during cooking. Add the caraway seeds and candied ginger and cook until the liquid has evaporated and the carrots have a nice, shiny glaze, about 10 minutes more. Stir and season to taste with salt and pepper.

1½ pounds carrots, trimmed, peeled, and cut diagonally into 2-inch pieces

4 tablespoons unsalted butter

1 teaspoon freshly grated orange zest

⅓ cup freshly squeezed orange juice

1 teaspoon caraway seeds

2 tablespoons finely chopped candied ginger

Salt and freshly ground black pepper

a peck of peppers

Colorful red and yellow bell peppers taste sweet when slowly stir-fried in the cast iron skillet. They make a good side dish with roast chicken and roast pork. The anchovies are a flavorful addition–they balance the sweet peppers with their saltiness. When red and yellow bell peppers are on sale at the market, you can make a double batch.

. . . .

MAKES 6 SERVINGS

* Heat the oil in a 10-inch cast iron skillet over high heat. Add all the peppers and stir-fry for 1 minute. Turn the heat down to medium low and cook for 6 to 8 minutes more. Stir in the vinegar, sprinkle with salt and pepper, and transfer to a shallow dish. Garnish with the anchovies and serve.

2 to 3 tablespoons olive oil

2 red bell peppers, seeded and cut into 1-inch squares

2 yellow bell peppers, seeded and cut into 1-inch squares

1 tablespoon red wine vinegar

Salt and freshly ground black pepper

6 anchovies, for garnish (optional)

mushroom, onion, and kale tuscan bread stew

The flavor of this dish reminds us of French onion soup without all the broth. It's hearty and makes the perfect side dish to fish, chicken, or pork. Great flavor with very little effort. Your guests will love it!

Note: If you opt to let the bread cubes "stale" overnight, start this prep the day before.

. . . .

MAKES 6 TO 8 SERVINGS

1 (12-ounce) loaf rustic bread, unsliced

2 tablespoons unsalted butter, divided

2 tablespoons olive oil, divided

1 shallot, minced

1½ cups sliced chanterelle or cremini mushrooms

1 yellow onion, coarsely chopped

2 cups kale, tough stems and ribs removed, cut into 1-inch strips

3 cups chicken broth

½ cup heavy cream

⅛ teaspoon ground or freshly grated nutmeg

2 teaspoons kosher salt

½ teaspoon freshly ground black pepper

1½ cups grated white cheddar, Gruyère, or fontina cheese

- Cut the bread into 1-inch cubes, enough to measure 6 cups, and place on a baking sheet. Either leave out overnight or lightly toast for 12 to 15 minutes in a preheated 350°F oven.

- When ready to make the stew, preheat the oven to 350°F (if toasting the bread, it can be done at this point).

- In a 10- or 12-inch cast iron skillet over medium heat, heat 1 tablespoon of the butter and 1 tablespoon of the olive oil. Add the shallot and cook for 2 minutes. Add the mushrooms and sauté for 5 minutes, or until mushrooms begin to brown. Transfer to a plate and set aside. Maintaining medium heat, add the remaining butter and olive oil to the pan, add the onions, and sauté for 5 minutes. Turn the heat to medium-low and cook for 10 minutes more. Add the shallots and mushrooms to the onions. Add the kale and ½ cup of the broth and gently toss. Add the bread cubes, the remaining broth, and the cream. Mix and turn gently to combine. Sprinkle with the nutmeg, salt, pepper, and cheese.

- Bake until the top is golden and inside the bread is soft but not too much liquid remains, 35 to 40 minutes. If the top is not browning, turn the heat up to 400°F and cook until golden brown. Remove from oven and let rest for 5 to 10 minutes before serving.

crispy red potatoes

Serve these creamy-on-the-inside, crispy-on-the-outside potatoes with roast chicken or lamb chops.

. . . .

MAKES 4 SERVINGS

- Preheat the oven to 400°F.

- Place the potatoes in a large pot. Cover with water and bring to a boil. Boil until easily pieced with a fork, 10 to 12 minutes. Drain and cool slightly. Swirl the oil in a 12-inch cast iron skillet. Cut the potatoes in half and place cut side down in the skillet. Bake until golden brown, about 20 minutes. Season with salt and pepper.

1½ pounds small red potatoes
2 tablespoons extra-virgin olive oil
Salt and freshly ground black pepper

quick stir-fried rice with oregon bay shrimp

Here's a good way to use leftover rice. You can make a fresh potful for this purpose, but you will want to chill it before cooking. We like to spice it up and add a dash of sriracha sauce to give the rice more heat. This dish is colorful and delicious!

Note: To make good fried rice, the ratio of water to rice when cooking is key. Rinse the rice three times, then for every cup of uncooked rice, add 1¼ cups water. Bring the water and rice to a boil, uncovered, in a large pot, turn down the heat to low, and then cover and let simmer for 20 minutes.

. . . .

MAKES 4 SERVINGS

- In a small bowl, combine the oyster sauce, and soy sauce. Set aside.

- Put the cooked rice in a large bowl and break it up with your fingers.

- Heat the vegetable oil in a 12-inch cast iron skillet over medium-high heat. Add the ginger and cook, stirring, for 15 seconds, then add the garlic, stir, and quickly add the rice to the skillet. Stir with a wooden spoon until the rice is heated through. Fold in the peas and pork, then stir in the egg.

- Stir the sauce mixture into the rice, add a few drops of sesame oil to taste, and combine well. Garnish with the green onions and shrimp. Serve with additional oyster and soy sauce.

2 tablespoons oyster sauce

2 tablespoons soy sauce

4 cups cold cooked rice

3 tablespoons vegetable oil

1 teaspoon minced ginger

1 clove garlic, minced

½ cup frozen green peas, thawed

½ cup diced barbecue pork

1 large egg, beaten

Sesame oil

¼ cup chopped green onions, for garnish

1 cup Oregon bay shrimp

tricolored vegetable cakes

This recipe makes for a fabulous side dish during the holidays or anytime. The cakes can be made smaller as an appetizer or larger as an accompaniment to chicken or pork; they also go well with game dishes. Frying them in ghee, the clarified butter that is a staple of cooking in South Asia, adds an authentic flavor of that region.

. . . .

MAKES 8 LARGE CAKES OR 12 SMALL CAKES

- Put the sweet potato in a medium pot of water and bring to a boil. Turn the heat down slightly and cook until just tender when pierced with a fork, about 10 minutes. Drain and allow to cool.

- Meanwhile, in a large bowl, grate the zucchini and the carrot using the largest openings of a box grater. When the sweet potato has cooled, grate in the same manner. Add the green onion, beaten egg, garam masala, salt, and pepper and mix.

- Add the ¼ cup flour and mix until combined. The mixture should be soft but hold together when shaped; if necessary, add the additional 1 tablespoon flour. With your hands, form into cakes. In a 10- to 12-inch cast iron skillet over medium heat, heat the ghee. Line a plate with paper towels.

- Add 4 or 5 cakes and cook until nicely golden brown, turning once, about 5 minutes on each side. Transfer to the paper towel–lined plate and repeat until all the cakes are cooked. Serve each cake with a dollop of sour cream and a dollop of lingonberry jam.

1 sweet potato, peeled and cut into thirds

1 zucchini, washed, ends trimmed

1 large carrot, peeled, ends trimmed

2 green onions, thinly sliced (about ¼ cup)

1 large egg, beaten

2 teaspoons Garam Masala (see page 56)

1 teaspoon kosher salt

¼ teaspoon freshly ground black pepper

¼ cup plus 1 tablespoon all-purpose flour

2 tablespoons ghee or vegetable oil

Sour cream

Lingonberry jam or another tart jam or cranberry sauce

roasted brussels sprouts and yukon gold potatoes with crispy pancetta

These little green cabbages are often passed over at the market. They have a wonderful flavor when cooked on the stove top or when roasted in the oven, and are then splashed with a little red wine vinegar and lemon juice to brighten the taste and color of the sprouts. Brussels sprouts should not be alone.

● ● ● ● ● ● ● ● ● ● ● ● ● ● ● ● ●

MAKES 4 TO 6 SERVINGS

- Put the potatoes in a large pot and fill with enough water to just cover them. Bring to a boil over medium-high heat and cook the potatoes until they are just tender, about 8 minutes. Drain and set aside.

- Heat a 10- or 12-inch cast iron skillet over medium heat. Add the pancetta and cook until crisp. Transfer to a small bowl. Add the brussels sprouts and broth to the skillet; cover with a lid or foil and simmer for 5 to 7 minutes. Remove the lid and continue simmering until the broth has evaporated. Add the olive oil, butter, and potatoes to the skillet and cook over medium-low heat until the brussels sprouts begin to brown. Gently stir in the cream. Cook for 2 minutes more. Sprinkle the pancetta over the vegetables; season with lemon juice, salt, and pepper; and serve.

3 to 4 Yukon Gold potatoes, peeled and cut into ½-inch cubes

½ cup diced pancetta or bacon

10 large brussels sprouts, ends trimmed, cut lengthwise into thirds

½ cup chicken broth or water

2 tablespoons extra-virgin olive oil

2 tablespoons unsalted butter

¼ cup heavy cream

2 teaspoons freshly squeezed lemon juice

Salt and freshly ground black pepper

skillet-baked polenta with white cheddar

The great virtue of this recipe, adapted from Paula Wolfert's cookbook *Mediterranean Grains and Greens*, is that it's baked in the oven, so it doesn't require the close attention and constant stirring of traditional polenta methods. We added the cheese to give the polenta its creamy texture.

. . . .

MAKES 6 SERVINGS

- Preheat the oven to 350°F.

- Butter a 12-inch cast iron skillet. Add the cornmeal, water, oil, and salt and stir until well mixed. Bake for 1 hour and 20 minutes. Stir the white cheddar and butter into the pot and bake for 10 minutes more. Let rest for several minutes. Season with salt and pepper to taste. Spoon into serving bowls and top each with 1 teaspoon butter.

2 cups medium coarse cornmeal

8 cups cold water

2 tablespoons extra-virgin olive oil

2 teaspoons salt

2 cups grated white cheddar cheese

4 tablespoons unsalted butter, plus 2 tablespoons for serving

Freshly ground black pepper

stir-fried green beans with ginger and ponzu

These green beans are a vegetable that even the kids love. The ginger and orange go so nicely together. Slightly crisp, they also make a great snack!

. . . .

MAKES 4 SERVINGS

- Bring a small pot of lightly salted water to a boil. Add the green beans and cook for 3 minutes. Drain and plunge into an ice water bath to stop the cooking process. Drain and pat dry.

- In a 10- to 12-inch cast iron skillet, heat the olive oil over medium heat. Add the ginger slices and swirl around in the oil briefly. Add the green beans and stir. Add the garlic, ponzu sauce, and orange zest, and stir to coat well. Cook for 3 minutes. Add the sesame oil and toss to coat. Remove from the heat and serve.

1½ pounds fresh green beans, trimmed

2 tablespoons olive oil

2 slices fresh ginger

1 clove garlic, sliced

3 tablespoons citrus ponzu sauce (see Resources on page 143) or substitute 2 tablespoons soy sauce and 1 tablespoon freshly squeezed orange juice

½ teaspoon freshly grated orange zest

½ teaspoon sesame oil

baking in the skillet

WE LOVE TO BAKE IN THE CAST IRON SKILLET. WE FIND THAT ANY BAKING RECIPE with cornmeal added turns out crispy and lightly browned on the outside and moist on the inside. ❙ The cast iron skillet acts like a hearth oven with its dry, even heat. Flatbreads, corn bread, upside-down cakes, and coffee cakes bake perfectly in the cast iron skillet. The skillet is also a great serving piece for presenting your lovely cakes, breads, or tarts. Crusts become golden and the fruit caramelizes beautifully. Turn the skillet upside-down and the bottom surface becomes the perfect pizza stone. You can bake pizzas and flatbreads in the oven, or outdoors in a hot skillet over an open fire or grill. The Spicy Apple Cake, served in the skillet in the middle of your picnic table on the Fourth of July, will be a standout. The skillet's simple, rustic quality makes everything you serve in it look and taste delicious!

welsh cakes

This recipe was given to us by our dear friend Mary Hanson, who lives in Seattle, and her daughter, Trish Richards, who lives in Cardiff, Wales. These little treats are so delicious and can be eaten warm or cold. Enjoy with a hot cup of tea!

• • • • • • • • • • • • • • • •

MAKES ABOUT 30 CAKES

- In a medium bowl, mix together the flour, salt, sugar, cinnamon, allspice, and nutmeg. Cut the butter into the flour mixture. Stir in the currants, egg, and milk. Mix with your fingers until just blended. On a lightly floured surface, roll out the dough to ¼ inch thick and cut out 2-inch rounds. Heat a 10- or 12-inch cast iron skillet over medium-high heat. Cook until lightly browned, about 3 minutes on each side. Transfer to a plate, sprinkle with sugar while still hot, and serve.

Scant 2 cups self-rising flour

¼ teaspoon salt

¼ cup super-fine sugar or granulated sugar

¼ teaspoon ground cinnamon

¼ teaspoon ground allspice

⅛ teaspoon freshly ground nutmeg

½ cup (1 stick) unsalted butter

¼ cup currants

1 large egg, beaten

2 tablespoons milk

Sugar, for sprinkling

pear almond cake

This best-of-season pear cake makes a good dessert, topped with whipped cream, or a warm, inviting Sunday morning coffee cake.

● ● ● ● ● ● ● ● ● ● ● ● ● ● ● ●

MAKES 8 SERVINGS

- Preheat the oven to 350°F.
- Cream together the butter and ¾ cup of the sugar until light and fluffy. Beat in the eggs, one at a time. Add the almond extract. Combine the flour, baking powder, and salt and add to the batter. Mix well. Butter a 10-inch cast iron skillet, spread the batter in an even layer in the bottom, and cover with the pears. Dot with the 2 teaspoons butter and sprinkle the remaining sugar over the top. Bake until golden, about 50 minutes.

10 tablespoons unsalted butter, at room temperature

1 cup sugar, divided

2 large eggs

½ teaspoon almond extract

1 cup all-purpose flour

½ teaspoon baking powder

½ teaspoon salt

3 Bartlett pears, peeled and diced into ½-by-¾-inch pieces

2 teaspoons cold unsalted butter

golden apple buckle

This moist, delicious apple dessert is truly a showstopper any time of the year. The apples fill the skillet, and the batter spreads over the fruit while baking.

. . . .

MAKES 8 SERVINGS

- Preheat the oven to 375°F.

- In a large bowl, mix the apples, sugar, flour, and melted butter. Spread the apples in a 10-inch cast iron skillet.

- To prepare the topping, cream the butter and sugar together until light and fluffy. Add the eggs, one at a time, along with the vanilla. Continue to beat for 1 to 2 minutes. Stir in the flour and baking powder.

- Spread the batter as evenly as possible over the apples. The batter will continue to spread during baking.

- Bake until golden, 45 to 50 minutes. Serve warm, topped with whipped cream. It's easy to reheat the dessert on top of the stove, over low heat.

FILLING

6 Golden Delicious or other sweet, crisp, juicy apples, peeled and cut into quarters, then sliced crosswise into 1/2-by-2-inch pieces

1/2 cup sugar

2 tablespoons all-purpose flour

1 tablespoon unsalted butter, melted

TOPPING

1/2 cup (1 stick) unsalted butter, at room temperature

1/2 cup sugar

2 large eggs

1 teaspoon vanilla extract

1 cup all-purpose flour

1 teaspoon baking powder

Whipped cream, for topping

cheddar cream scones

Serve these golden cheese-topped scones with raspberry jam, sausages, and a platter of fresh fruit for breakfast on a sleepy Sunday morning.

. . . .

MAKES 10 SCONES

- Preheat the oven to 425°F. Generously butter a 12-inch cast iron skillet, and flour a surface well for shaping the dough.

- In a large bowl, combine the flour, sugar, and baking powder. Cut in the butter using a pastry cutter or with your fingers. Stir in 1 cup of the cheese. Make a well in the center of the dough and pour in the egg and cream. Mix until the dough just comes together.

2½ cups self-rising flour

2 tablespoons sugar

1 tablespoon baking powder

¼ cup (½ stick) cold unsalted butter, cut into small pieces

1½ cups grated cheddar cheese, divided

1 large egg, beaten

1¼ cups heavy cream

- Gather the dough into a ball and turn out onto the floured surface. Knead the dough several times, adding more flour if the dough is too wet. Roll or pat the dough into a circle ½ to ¾ inch thick. Cut the circle into 10 triangles. Transfer the scones to the buttered skillet, leaving ¼ inch between each scone. Sprinkle with the remaining ½ cup cheese. Bake until golden brown, 25 to 30 minutes. Serve warm.

caramel apple crisp

There are many apple crisp recipes out there, but this one has just the right combination of filling with apples, and a golden, crunchy topping that only a cast iron skillet can produce. Serve warm with vanilla ice cream.

. . . .

MAKES 6 SERVINGS

- Preheat the oven to 350°F.

- To prepare the topping, combine the flour, oats, brown sugar, and cinnamon. With your fingers, cut in the butter until the mixture is nice and crumbly.

- In a 10-inch cast iron skillet over medium heat, cook the butter and granulated sugar together just until it bubbles and starts to turn golden, about 5 minutes. Stir in the apples. Sprinkle the lemon juice and oatmeal topping evenly over the apples. Bake for 1 hour.

CRISP TOPPING

1 cup all-purpose flour

1 cup old-fashioned rolled oats

1 cup brown sugar

1 teaspoon ground cinnamon

¾ cup (1½ sticks) unsalted butter, cut into 8 pieces

FILLING

4 tablespoons unsalted butter

4 tablespoons granulated sugar

6 Jonagold or other firm, sweet, juicy apples, peeled, quartered, and cut crosswise into ½-inch slices

1 tablespoon freshly squeezed lemon juice

fresh rhubarb and huckleberry tart

You can use different fruits with this recipe. We like apples and rhubarb together or plums when they are in season. If you can't find wild huckleberries, strawberries also complement the rhubarb nicely. This is such a great dough and is very forgiving. The sour cream keeps the dough moist, while the cornmeal gives it a crispy texture.

• • • • • • • • • • • • • • • •

MAKES 6 TO 8 SERVINGS

- To prepare the filling, in a large bowl, add the rhubarb, huckleberries, and sugar and toss to coat. Let sit for 15 minutes. Pour off and reserve ¼ cup of the rhubarb liquid. Add the cornstarch and lemon juice to the fruit and toss to coat. Set aside.

- To prepare the glaze, in a small saucepan over medium-low heat, heat the ¼ cup rhubarb liquid and strawberry jam and as it heats up, stir to combine. When the jam has become more liquid, about 5 minutes, remove from the heat and set aside.

- To prepare the pastry, preheat the oven to 400°F.

- In a small bowl, combine the sour cream and ice-cold water.

- In a medium bowl, combine the flour, cornmeal, sugar, and salt. Add half of the butter and coat well with the flour mixture. Add the remaining butter and coat well with the flour mixture. Mix with your hands or a pastry cutter or food processor until the pieces of butter are pea-sized (about 8 to 10 seconds in the food processor). Add the sour cream mixture, 1 tablespoon at a time, gently mixing after each addition. Once all the liquid has been incorporated, form the dough into a disk.

FILLING

1 pound rhubarb, chopped ½-inch thick (about 5½ cups)

½ cup fresh or frozen (thawed) wild huckleberries

¾ cup sugar

3 tablespoons cornstarch

2 teaspoons freshly squeezed lemon juice

GLAZE

¼ cup rhubarb-sugar liquid from filling

3 tablespoons strawberry jam

PASTRY

¼ cup sour cream

⅓ cup ice-cold water

1½ cups all-purpose flour, plus 2 to 3 tablespoons for rolling

⅓ cup cornmeal

1 tablespoon sugar

½ teaspoon salt

10 tablespoons cold unsalted butter, cut into small pieces, plus additional for buttering the skillet

2 tablespoons raw (turbinado) sugar, for sprinkling

- Lightly dust a cutting board with flour and lightly butter a 10- or 12-inch cast iron skillet. Roll out the dough, lightly dusting the top of the dough if it starts to stick, to form a 14-inch disk. Fold the dough over the rolling pin and transfer to the skillet. Carefully lay flat in the skillet; there will be extra dough, which you can let overlap until the fruit is added. With a slotted spoon, transfer the fruit to the center of the skillet, working your way out and lifting the edge of the dough so the fruit flows under it. (There will be extra liquid left in the bottom of the bowl; you can save this syrup for later use on pancakes—just heat and serve.) After adding all the filling, spread it out evenly, lifting the dough at the edges and laying it back down on top of the fruit. You will have a 3-inch border to overlap all the way around. With a spoon, drizzle ¼ cup of the glaze evenly over the top of the fruit.

- Sprinkle the raw sugar on the exposed, overlapping crust and bake until the crust is golden, 30 to 35 minutes. Serve warm with vanilla ice cream.

caramelized onion piadina with chèvre and kalamata olives

Piadina is a thin Italian flatbread that is similar to focaccia but thinner and round. Turning the cast iron skillet upside down and baking on the bottom of the skillet is like baking in a hearth oven! This bread is tender and light–a nice change from chewy, tough crusts. As you remove the piadina from the oven, spread it with butter and apricot jam for a delectable treat.

• • • • • • • • • • • • • • • • •

MAKES 6 SERVINGS

- Preheat the oven to 450°F.

- To prepare the crust, dissolve the yeast in the warm water, add the sugar, and let sit for 5 minutes. Stir in the salt, flour, and olive oil. Mix well. Flour a board generously and knead the dough on it for several minutes, until the dough forms a smooth ball. Place in a bowl and cover with plastic wrap. Let rest for 30 minutes in a warm place. Meanwhile, prepare the topping.

- Heat the butter in a 12-inch cast iron skillet over medium heat. Add the onion, thyme, and sugar and cook until golden, about 8 minutes. Transfer to a bowl and set aside.

- Clean the skillet. Turn upside down and brush with olive oil. When the dough is ready, flour a board well and roll out the dough into a circle the size of the skillet. Place the dough on the oiled skillet bottom and spoon the onions evenly over the dough, leaving a 1-inch border. Sprinkle evenly with the chèvre and olives. Bake until golden, 20 to 25 minutes. Sprinkle with sea salt and serve.

CRUST

1 (¼-ounce) package active dry yeast

¾ cup warm water

1 teaspoon sugar

1 teaspoon salt

1½ cups all-purpose flour

3 tablespoons extra-virgin olive oil

CARAMELIZED ONION TOPPING

2 tablespoons unsalted butter

1 sweet yellow onion, cut in half, then thinly sliced crosswise

1 teaspoon chopped fresh thyme

1 teaspoon sugar

2 ounces chèvre, crumbled

¼ cup chopped kalamata olives

Sea salt

moist skillet corn bread

This corn bread is so moist, with a crispy crust. We recommend finely ground cornmeal such as Alber's brand. Our family's favorite way to eat this corn bread is with a simple honey butter.

Variations: Add ⅔ cup fresh corn when it's in season. If you like an even spicier corn bread, add ½ cup pepper jack cheese. You can also add 2 teaspoons chopped rosemary and 1 teaspoon fresh thyme to your dry ingredients.

. . . .

MAKES 8 SERVINGS

- Preheat the oven to 400°F.

- Position a rack in the center of the oven. Generously butter the sides and bottom of a 10- to 12-inch cast iron skillet. In a large bowl, whisk together the cornmeal, flour, baking powder, baking soda, sugar, salt, and chili powder. In a medium bowl, whisk together the eggs, sour cream, half-and-half, and 4 tablespoons of the melted butter (cooled slightly). Add the egg mixture to the cornmeal mixture and stir just until combined. Do not overmix.

1 cup finely ground yellow cornmeal
1 cup all-purpose flour
1½ teaspoons baking powder
½ teaspoon baking soda
2 tablespoons sugar
½ teaspoon salt
½ teaspoon chili powder
2 large eggs
½ cup sour cream
1¼ cups half-and-half
6 tablespoons unsalted butter, melted, divided
Honey butter, for serving

- Heat the skillet over medium heat. Pour the cornmeal batter into the hot skillet, jiggling the skillet slightly to level out the batter.

- Bake in the oven for 10 minutes. Quickly but carefully remove the skillet from the oven and drizzle the remaining 2 tablespoons melted butter over the top. Return to the oven and continue baking until golden brown and an inserted toothpick comes out clean, about 8 minutes more. Cool, cut into wedges, and serve with honey butter.

marionberry cornmeal coffee cake

We love to pick fresh berries in August. In the Northwest we are fortunate to have many varieties of berries. One of our favorites is the marionberry, because it's a large, firm berry with small sacs, which makes it the perfect baking berry.

. . . .

MAKES 8 SERVINGS

- Preheat oven to 375°F.

- In a large bowl, mix together the flour, cornmeal, orange zest, baking powder, salt, and 1 cup of sugar. In a medium bowl, whisk together the eggs, sour cream, and milk. Then whisk in the melted butter. Add the flour mixture and mix until just combined. Do not overmix.

- Heat a 10-inch cast iron skillet. Add the 1 tablespoon butter. Swirl to cover the pan's interior. Spread the batter evenly in the skillet. Sprinkle the berries over the top. In a small bowl, combine the remaining sugar and the cinnamon and sprinkle over the top.

- Bake until light golden brown, about 45 minutes.

1¼ cups all-purpose flour
½ cup yellow cornmeal
1 teaspoon freshly grated orange zest
2 teaspoons baking powder
1 teaspoon salt
1⅓ cups sugar, divided
2 large eggs
¼ cup sour cream
¼ cup milk
1 stick (½ cup) unsalted butter, melted
1 tablespoon unsalted butter
3 cups berries, preferably marionberries
1 teaspoon ground cinnamon

king's bread

This is an easy yeast bread that makes wonderful toast. It bakes to a golden brown in the cast iron skillet. Slice thinly and serve with cheese and fresh fruit.

. . . .

MAKES 6 SERVINGS

1 tablespoon active dry yeast

1 tablespoon sugar

¼ cup warm water

6 tablespoons unsalted butter, melted, divided

2 large eggs, beaten

¾ cup milk, warmed

2¾ cups all-purpose flour

- Preheat the oven to 375°F. Flour a board well and generously butter a 10-inch cast iron skillet.

- In a small bowl, dissolve the yeast and sugar in the warm water and let proof for 5 minutes. In a large mixing bowl, combine the dissolved yeast, 5 tablespoons of the melted butter, eggs, milk, and flour. Turn out onto the floured board and knead until a smooth ball forms, 3 to 5 minutes. Place in the skillet and flatten into an 8-inch circle. Cover with plastic wrap and let rise in a warm spot in your kitchen for 1 hour.

- Brush the top of the bread with the remaining melted butter. Bake until golden, 25 to 30 minutes.

rosemary parmesan flatbread

Baking in the cast iron skillet creates a crusty, golden flatbread. You can get creative and add an assortment of toppings. Some of our favorites are grilled vegetables, oven-roasted tomatoes, and fromage blanc. You can also try smoked salmon and herbed cream cheese.

. . . .

MAKES 6 SERVINGS

- Preheat oven to 400°F.

- In a small bowl, combine the garlic and olive oil and set aside.

- In a medium bowl, dissolve the yeast in the warm water. Add the sugar and let rest for 5 minutes. Add the egg to the yeast mixture. Gently stir. Stir in the salt and flour, adding ½ cup at a time, until a soft dough forms. Shape into a ball and turn out onto a lightly floured surface. Knead until nice and smooth. Turn the mixing bowl upside down over the dough and let rest for 5 minutes.

2 cloves garlic, minced
¼ cup extra-virgin olive oil
1 tablespoon active dry yeast
⅓ cup warm water
¼ teaspoon sugar
1 large egg, beaten
½ teaspoon kosher salt
1½ cups all-purpose flour
1 tablespoon unsalted butter
1 tablespoon chopped fresh rosemary
⅓ cup freshly grated Parmesan cheese
1 teaspoon sea salt

- Meanwhile, melt the butter in a 10-inch cast iron skillet. Roll the dough out into a 10-inch circle and transfer to the skillet. Brush with the olive oil mixture and sprinkle with the rosemary, cheese, and sea salt. Let rise for 30 minutes. Bake until golden brown, 15 to 17 minutes. Serve warm.

cinnamon cream roll-ups with orange glaze

These no-yeast rolls are quick to fix. The self-rising flour makes a soft dough, and the cinnamon filling drips down during baking and caramelizes in the skillet. They taste so old-fashioned and yummy!

. . . .

MAKES 6 TO 8 SERVINGS

- Preheat the oven to 425°F and butter a 12-inch cast iron skillet.

- To prepare the filling, in a small bowl, combine all the ingredients. Reserve.

- To prepare the dough, lightly flour a surface for kneading. In a large bowl, combine the self-rising flour and sugar. Pour in the cream and the melted butter and stir until well blended; the dough will be a little stiff. Knead the dough briefly on the floured surface. Roll out into a rectangle, 8 by 12 inches. Spread evenly with the filling, leaving a 1-inch border around the edges. Roll up the dough like a jelly roll, and cut into 8, 2-inch-wide slices. Arrange in the skillet and bake until golden, 20 to 25 minutes.

- Meanwhile, in a small bowl, blend the powdered sugar and orange juice until smooth. Spread the glaze over the top of the warm rolls and serve.

FILLING

1 cup brown sugar

2 teaspoons ground cinnamon

4 tablespoons unsalted butter, melted

DOUGH

2½ cups self-rising flour

2 tablespoons granulated sugar

1¼ cups cream

6 tablespoons unsalted butter, melted

GLAZE

1 cup powdered sugar

¼ cup orange juice or heavy cream

grammy's oatmeal cake with coconut pecan frosting

This recipe has been passed down through three generations; it is the perfect picnic cake and a favorite on the Fourth of July. This cake is very moist, and the coconut-brown sugar frosting is so good with the oatmeal texture.

. . . .

MAKES 6 TO 8 SERVINGS

- Preheat the oven to 350°F.

- Butter a 10-inch cast iron skillet. In a medium bowl, add the oatmeal and pour the boiling water over it. Mix and let cool.

- In a large mixing bowl, cream together the butter and the brown and granulated sugars. Add the eggs, one at a time, beating thoroughly after each addition. Sift in the flour, baking soda, cinnamon, nutmeg, and salt. Stir in the cooled oatmeal mixture. Pour the batter into the pan and bake until firm in the center, 30 to 35 minutes. Spread the Coconut Pecan Frosting on the cake while it is still warm.

1 cup oatmeal

1½ cups boiling water

½ cup (1 stick) unsalted butter

1 cup packed brown sugar

1 cup granulated sugar

2 large eggs

1½ cups all-purpose flour

1 teaspoon baking soda

1 teaspoon ground cinnamon

¼ teaspoon freshly grated nutmeg

½ teaspoon salt

Coconut Pecan Frosting (recipe follows)

coconut pecan frosting

MAKES 1½ CUPS

- Preheat the broiler.

- Combine all the ingredients and mix well. Spoon the mixture over the cake and spread carefully and evenly. Place the cake under the broiler until the topping starts to bubble and the coconut starts to brown, 2 to 3 minutes.

3 tablespoons unsalted butter, melted

⅓ cup packed brown sugar

½ cup shredded, sweetened coconut

½ cup coarsely chopped pecans

2 tablespoons milk

½ teaspoon vanilla extract

skillet chocolate pudding cake

This old-fashioned dessert will please all chocolate lovers. A combination of pudding and cake, it makes its own sauce. After baking, let the cake rest for ten minutes before serving, or make ahead of time and when you are ready to serve, warm it on the stove top over low heat.

• • • • • • • • • • • • • • • •

MAKES 8 SERVINGS

- Preheat the oven to 375°F.

- Put the flour, sugar, cocoa, baking powder, and salt into a large bowl and stir until well blended. Add the half-and-half, melted butter, and vanilla. Mix until a stiff batter forms. Place a 10-inch cast iron skillet in the oven to heat for 5 minutes. Remove from the oven. Swirl the butter in the warm skillet to coat it fairly evenly. Pour the batter into the skillet, and don't worry if it is a bit uneven.

- Meanwhile, combine the water and sugar in a small saucepan. Bring to a boil. Pour over the batter. Don't stir. Bake until the cake is firm to the touch, about 30 minutes. Serve warm topped with whipped cream.

1 cup all-purpose flour

¾ cup sugar

½ cup unsweetened cocoa

2 teaspoons baking powder

¼ teaspoon salt

1 cup half-and-half

5 tablespoons unsalted butter, melted

1 teaspoon vanilla extract

1 tablespoon unsalted butter

1½ cups water

1½ cups sugar

Whipped cream, for serving

peach blueberry cornmeal cobbler

We have adapted a recipe given to us by Jude Russell, chef/instructor for Metropolitan Markets in Seattle. This delicious summer cobbler can be served for brunch or dessert.

• • • • • • • • • • • • • • • • • •

MAKES 8 SERVINGS

- Preheat the oven to 375°F.

- In a 10-inch cast iron skillet over medium heat, melt the butter with ¾ cup of the brown sugar. Stir until the sugar is melted, then stir in the blueberries and peaches and remove from the heat.

- In a medium mixing bowl, stir together the cornmeal, flour, baking powder, and salt.

- In the electric mixer bowl, beat the eggs and the remaining brown sugar until light and fluffy. Beat in the melted butter and vanilla. Fold in the cornmeal and flour mixture until well combined.

4 tablespoons unsalted butter
1½ cups light brown sugar, divided
2 cups blueberries
3 cups sliced peaches or nectarines
½ cup yellow cornmeal
1 cup all-purpose flour
1 teaspoon baking powder
¼ teaspoon salt
3 large eggs, at room temperature
4 tablespoons unsalted butter, melted
2 teaspoons vanilla extract
Lightly sweetened whipped cream, for topping

- Spoon the batter over the fruit mixture in the skillet and smooth out the top with a spatula. Bake until the cake springs back when touched, 30 to 40 minutes. Serve warm, topped with the whipped cream.

roasted pears with double chocolate fudge sauce

This dessert bakes to perfection in the cast iron skillet because it cooks the pears so evenly. If you need a quick and easy dessert, this works well. You can also use caramel sauce, or offer guests a choice.

. . . .

MAKES 6 SERVINGS

- Preheat the oven to 375°F.

- Cut the pears in half lengthwise. Do not peel. With a melon baller, remove the center core, leaving a small cavity. Cut a slice off the underside so the fruit will be stable when laid with the cavity facing up. Place the pears in a 10-inch cast iron skillet. Put 1 teaspoon each of butter and sugar in each cavity. Bake for 30 minutes. Serve warm with vanilla ice cream and Double Chocolate Fudge Sauce.

3 Bartlett pears, ripe but still firm
6 teaspoons unsalted butter
6 teaspoons brown sugar
Vanilla ice cream
Double Chocolate Fudge Sauce (recipe follows)

double chocolate fudge sauce

This is a favorite recipe from our good friends Sally and Larry Brown. Delectable with roasted pears, it's also terrific over roasted bananas—or vanilla ice cream. We also like it for dipping strawberries.

• • • • • • • • • • • • • • • • •

MAKES 2 CUPS

- Combine the sugar, cocoa, cream, and corn syrup in a heavy saucepan. Slowly bring to a boil, stirring to dissolve the sugar. Lower the heat and simmer, uncovered, for 5 minutes, stirring often.

- Remove from the heat and add the chopped chocolate and butter, stirring until melted and smooth. Stir in the vanilla.

⅔ cup sugar

½ cup unsweetened Dutch-process cocoa

¾ cup heavy cream

½ cup light corn syrup

4 ounces unsweetened dark chocolate, chopped

5 tablespoons unsalted butter

2 teaspoons vanilla extract

spicy apple cake

The best recipes are your friends' favorites. Our good friend Gretchen Mathers gave us this recipe many years ago, and it's become one of our favorite recipes for fall, when fresh apples are abundant and sweet spices warm us on chilly days. This cake is fast and easy to make–no laborious apple peeling–and it needs no frosting; it is moist and scrumptious all on its own. Serve it plain for brunch or as a dessert topped with vanilla ice cream and warm caramel sauce.

· · · · · · · · · · · · · · · ·

MAKES 8 SERVINGS

- Preheat the oven to 325°F.

- In a large bowl, combine the apples and sugar. Let sit for one hour. In a small bowl, soak the raisins in the rum. Meanwhile, butter a 10-inch cast iron skillet.

- In a large mixing bowl, combine the sugared apples, rum-soaked raisins (with any remaining rum), oil, eggs, vanilla, and walnuts.

- Combine the flour, baking soda, salt, cinnamon, cloves, and nutmeg. Add to the apple mixture and mix well. Pour into the skillet. Bake until golden brown and firm to the touch, 45 to 50 minutes.

4 cups chopped Jonagold or other sweet, crisp, juicy apples, unpeeled

2 cups sugar

1 cup golden raisins

¼ cup rum

½ cup vegetable oil

2 eggs, beaten

2 teaspoons vanilla extract

1 cup chopped walnuts

2 cups all-purpose flour

1½ teaspoons baking soda

1 teaspoon salt

2 teaspoons ground cinnamon

½ teaspoon ground cloves

1 teaspoon freshly grated nutmeg

fennel salt–crusted rolls

A popular Middle Eastern treat is pita bread dipped first in olive oil, then in a cone filled with different spice and nut blends (such as *dukkah*). We adapted this idea in a very simple combo: fennel and salt, on lightly oiled rolls. This finishing salt is also great on pork or chicken. Try different spice blends to give your own homemade rolls a twist. These rolls don't need butter, but a little honey sure is nice!

• • • • • • • • • • • • • • • • •

MAKES 16 ROLLS

- In a large bowl, dissolve the yeast in the warm water. Let rest until the yeast begins to foam, about 5 minutes. Meanwhile, lightly flour a surface for kneading the dough.

- In a small saucepan, warm the milk over medium-high heat, stirring occasionally, until it is hot and small bubbles form around the edge of the pan. Turn the heat down to medium and simmer for 2 to 3 minutes more. Remove from the heat, then stir in the butter and sugar. Allow the milk to cool to room temperature.

1 (¼-ounce) package active dry yeast

¼ cup warm water

1 cup milk

3 tablespoons unsalted butter, softened

2 tablespoons sugar

1 large egg, beaten

1 teaspoon kosher salt

3¼ cups all-purpose flour

3 tablespoons plus ½ teaspoon olive oil, divided

FENNEL SALT

2 tablespoons fennel seeds

1 teaspoon sea salt

- Add the milk mixture to the yeast and whisk until combined, about 30 seconds. Whisk in the egg, salt, and 1 cup of the flour until combined. Add another 1 cup flour and mix until combined. Add the third cup of flour and work in with a spatula; it will be a very sticky, wet dough. Work the dough into a ball and turn it out onto the floured surface. Clean and lightly oil the bowl with ½ teaspoon of the oil.

- Lightly flour your hands and the top of the dough and knead for 6 to 7 minutes, turning a quarter turn and folding the dough on top of itself, then pushing down with the heel of your hand. Continue kneading until the dough is smooth and elastic, working in the additional flour only if the dough is really sticking. When you pinch the dough and it springs back, you know your dough has the elasticity that it needs. Form the dough into a ball and place it in the oiled bowl. Drape a towel over the top and place in a warm spot until the dough has doubled in size, 1 to 1½ hours.

- In a small skillet over medium heat, toast the fennel seeds, stirring until they release their fragrant aroma and turn just faintly brown, about 3 minutes. Add to a mortar and pestle or a spice grinder, and crush or pulse until finely ground. Pour into a small bowl and stir in the sea salt.

- Preheat the oven to 425°F.

- Lightly oil a 10- or 12-inch cast iron skillet with 1 tablespoon of the oil. Punch down the dough and form into 2-inch balls, filling the skillet with 12 rolls about 1 inch apart. Brush each roll lightly with ½ teaspoon olive oil and sprinkle with 1 teaspoon fennel salt. Cover with a towel and let rise for another 30 to 35 minutes.

- When the rolls have risen, bake until the tops are golden brown, 20 to 25 minutes. Repeat with any remaining dough. Serve warm.

dessert pancakes with grand marnier and huckleberry sauce

You can make the pancakes and the filling ahead of time. Add the filling just before serving and warm the pancakes slowly in the skillet over medium-low heat.

• • • • • • • • • • • • • • • •

MAKES 8 SERVINGS

- To prepare the filling, in a medium bowl, whisk all the ingredients together until smooth. Cover with plastic wrap and refrigerate until ready to serve.

- To prepare the pancakes, add the eggs, milk, Grand Marnier, salt, flour, and melted butter into a blender and process briefly. Alternatively, whisk together in a large bowl until well blended.

- Warm a 10-inch cast iron skillet over medium heat. Brush the skillet with the oil. Pour in ⅓ cup batter and swirl to cover the skillet evenly. Cook for 1½ to 2 minutes, until lightly golden, then turn over and cook 1 minute longer. Transfer to the parchment paper. Repeat with the remaining batter, brushing the pan lightly with more oil before adding batter.

- Place 2 tablespoons filling in the center of each pancake. Fold in half, then in half again, forming a triangle. Heat the syrup, warm the pancakes in the skillet over medium-low heat, and serve.

MASCARPONE FILLING

⅓ cup sugar

⅓ cup mascarpone cheese

⅓ cup crème fraîche

2 tablespoons cream cheese

1 teaspoon orange zest

2 tablespoons Grand Marnier (or other orange-flavored liqueur or orange juice)

PANCAKES

3 large eggs

1¾ cups whole milk

2 tablespoons Grand Marnier (or other orange-flavored liqueur or orange juice)

½ teaspoon salt

1 cup all-purpose flour

2 tablespoons unsalted butter, melted

3 tablespoons vegetable oil

8 (12-inch) squares parchment paper

Huckleberry sauce or blueberry syrup

resources

Crate & Barrel
www.crateandbarrel.com

Foraged and Found Edibles
www.foragedandfoundedibles.com
Wild foods, from mushrooms to wild greens, freshly picked with care

Lodge Cast Iron
www.lodgemfg.com

More Than Gourmet
www.morethangourmet.com
800-860-9385
French demi-glace

Select Gourmet
www.selectgourmetfoods.com

The Spanish Table
www.spanishtable.com
1426 Western Avenue, Seattle, WA 98101
206-682-2827

Sur La Table
www.surlatable.com

Tom Douglas Rubs
www.tomdouglas.com
2030 Fifth Avenue, Seattle, WA 98121
206-448-2001

Uwajimaya
www.uwajimaya.com
Ponzu sauces, black rice wine vinegar, chow fun noodles, furikake seasonings, and other Asian specialty products

World Spice Merchants
www.worldspice.com
1509 Western Avenue, Seattle, WA 98101
206-682-7274
Spices and spice blends

index

about the authors

SHARON KRAMIS (left) is the author of four cookbooks, including *Berries: A Country Garden Cookbook* and *Northwest Bounty,* and coauthor of *The Cast Iron Skillet Cookbook* and *The Dutch Oven Cookbook.* A Northwest native, she holds a degree in food science from the University of Washington and is a former food writer for the *Mercer Island Reporter.* Sharon studied with legendary cooking figure James Beard at his summer cooking school in Seaside, Oregon, for six years. She is a founding member of the International Association of Culinary Professionals and Les Dames d'Escoffier's Seattle chapter. She continues to participate in menu development for Anthony's Restaurants in the Northwest. She lives with her husband, Larry, on Hammersley Inlet in South Puget Sound.

JULIE KRAMIS HEARNE (right) is coauthor of *The Cast Iron Skillet Cookbook* and *The Dutch Oven Cookbook.* She was brought up with a love of food, and has always enjoyed cooking and learning about food. Julie attended Seattle Pacific University for a degree in education, but after taking a food science class she realized where her true passion lay. Julie opened two restaurants with her husband, Harker.

She has taken ongoing classes at the Culinary Institute of America in Napa Valley, and spent a year training with Jerry Traunfeld at the nationally renowned Herbfarm Restaurant in Woodinville, Washington. Julie is a member of Les Dames d'Escoffier's Seattle chapter and currently teaches cooking classes, works as a consultant, and raises her three boys with her husband in Seattle, Washington. For more information, visit her website: www.whatsjuliecooking.com.

Sharon and Julie are either reading about food, cooking, or trying new foods and always learning something along the way.